Animation Development

FROM PITCH TO PRODUCTION

by David B. Levy

ALLWORTH PRESS
NEW YORK

School of
VISUAL ARTS

13   12   11   10   09   5   4   3   2   1

Published by Allworth Press
An imprint of Allworth Communications, Inc.
10 East 23rd Street, New York, NY 10010

Cover design by Tamara Gildengers Connolly
Interior design by Tamara Gildengers Connolly
Page composition/typography by Sharp Des!gns, Lansing, Michigan
Cover images: *Codename: Kids Next Door* and all related characters and elements are trademarks of and © Cartoon Network, A Time Warner company. *Super Why!* image is © 2008 Out of the Blue Enterprises, LLC. All rights reserved. *Super Why* is a registered trademark and all related titles, logos, and characters are trademarks of Out of the Blue Enterprises, LLC. *SpongeBob SquarePants* art is © 2008 Viacom International, Inc. All rights reserved. Nickelodeon, SpongeBob SquarePants, and all related titles, logos, and characters are trademarks of Viacom International, Inc. Created by Stephen Hillenburg.

ISBN-13: 978-1-58115-661-4
ISBN-10: 1-58115-661-8

LIBRARY OF CONGRESS CATALOGING-IN-PUBLICATION DATA
Levy, David B.
Animation development : from pitch to production / by David B. Levy.
    p. cm.
Includes index.
ISBN 978-1-58115-661-4
1. Animation (Cinematography)—Vocational guidance. 2. Animated films—Vocational guidance. 3. Television—Vocational guidance. I. Title.
NC1765.L476 2009
791.43'34023—dc22
2009011226

Printed in the United States of America

Dedication

A hundred years ago, animation was a novelty running side by side with the emergence of motion pictures. It was not until the development of the animated series, which featured a recurring star character, that animation's place in the entertainment industry achieved any kind of permanence. The series format allowed its creators the luxury of developing a character over an extended period of time. Felix the Cat may have debuted in the 1919 cartoon *Feline Follies*, but it was not until a couple of years later that the character would resemble the cat we still know and love today. Over the course of many shorts helmed by creator Otto Messmer, Felix gained his appealing, streamlined, circular design and developed his pantomime-perfect personality. One can see the same process of evolution occur over and over again in animation history, from Bugs Bunny to Homer Simpson. I dedicate this book to all of the brilliant creators, writers, storyboard artists, layout artists, designers, background artists, animators, directors, editors, composers, voice artists, and sound designers of the past, present, and future, who—over each episodic outing—help to sharpen a series to animated perfection. Each episode is not only one more chance to get it right; it's another chance to make history.

Table of Contents

Acknowledgments

Oh, the irony. For more than ten years, I navigated the wilds of animation pitching and development, only to find my first success scoring a greenlight, not for a TV pilot or series, but for a book project (*Your Career in Animation: How to Survive and Thrive*). Go figure. I've come to see this as an allegory for the subject of animation pitching and development. Success often arrives in unexpected ways and on a time line all its own.

But there's nothing random about the help, support, encouragement, and inspiration I've received during my attempt to cut a Lewis and Clark–style trail through this industry. Special thanks go to Linda Simensky, Fred Seibert, and Brown Johnson for providing my earliest opportunities to pitch. My deepest gratitude is extended towards Paula Rosenthal for awarding me my first TV development deal (which conveniently arrived early in the writing process of this book), and for parlaying me into the next level of my career as a script/development writer on a subsequent TV property.

This book would be noticeably thinner and less nutritious without the generous support and contributions of some of today's top creators. I'm forever indebted to Carl W. Adams, Craig Bartlett, Jerry Beck, Loren Bouchard, John R. Dilworth, David Fine, Manny Galan, Alan Goodman, Carl H. Greenblatt, Butch Hartman, Stephen Hillenburg, Jim Jinkins, Traci Paige Johnson, Fran Krause, Diane Kredensor, Candy Kugel, Craig McCracken, Adam Peltzman, Janet Perlman, Jackson Publick, Debra Solomon, Amy Steinberg, Doug TenNapel, Tom Warburton, and Mo Willems.

No less important to this book project, let alone to the process of animation pitching and development, were these kind folks from the ranks of network and Web development. Three cheers to Alice Cahn, Eric Coleman, Peter Gal, Athena Georgaklis, Eric Homan, Brown Johnson, Heather Kenyon, Madeleine Lévesque, Alex Manugian, Megan O'Neill, Fred Seibert, Linda Simensky, and Tara Sorensen. A round of applause to entertainment lawyers Robert D. Marcus and Jim Arnoff for explaining complicated legal issues in terms so simple, even a four-year-old could understand. (The reader is encouraged to consult a four-year-old for the translation.)

Finally, special thanks to my wife, Deborah M. Staab, who, with her question, "What's your next book?," presumed that I had another in me, thus leading me on the road to writing this book that might help you have a better shot at successfully developing, pitching, and producing your creations. Debbie's next question, "Do you want mustard on that?" has proved less influential on my destiny, but infinitely more delicious.

Introduction

> "This is not for the faint of heart."
>
> — **Madeleine Lévesque, executive vice president of content development, 9 Story Entertainment**

I'm sitting here typing away in my underwear contemplating the reader-ship of this book. Why underwear? Well, I'd like this to be an intimate read, and it just so happens to be a humid New York summer day. As for subjects, I don't think I could have chosen a more difficult one. I was recently chatting with my friend, veteran development executive Linda Simensky, telling her a curious story in which, for a moment, it looked like my hard-won (now, there's an understatement) development deal had been squashed. Her reaction both horrified and comforted me: "I don't know how anything gets made," she said.

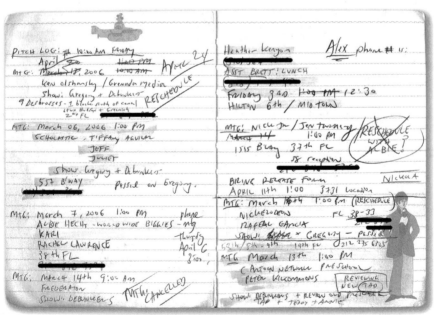

Pages from my journal logging two months of pitch meetings from spring 2006. Luckily, they don't award pitches based on ability to stay in the lines.

Before the folks at Allworth Press were ready to greenlight this book, they needed assurance that I would not ignore the emotional roller coaster that is so inherent in the pitch process. They needn't have worried. In my ten years of writing, creating, and pitching, I've had more highs and lows than the streets of San Francisco. Encounters with rude executives? Check. Getting strung along for six months for a promised greenlight that never quite materialized? Check. Flat-out rejections? Check. Being on the wrong side of industry trends and fads? Check. Being offered unfair deals? Check. Waiting months and years for an answer on a pitch? Check. Never even getting an answer? Check.

I'd be a fool or a liar if I said that these experiences didn't sometimes make me want to pack up and run. In some ways it felt like I was banging my head against the wall for ten years, hoping for a different result each time. Yet what happened to me only tells half the story. There is another set of questions that are a lot harder to answer: Did I ever pitch a half-baked idea? Check. Did I ever pitch with substandard artwork instead of bringing in others to help me? Check. Did I resist bringing in seasoned collaborators who might have improved my projects? Check. Did I pitch ideas not created from the heart, just for the sake of pitching? Check. Did I pitch to networks that catered to audiences to whom I could not or did not relate? Check. Did I ever lose my temper during a frustrating pitch meeting? Check. Did I have to make some mistakes over and over again before finally learning from them? Check.

You might be asking yourself, if I pitched year after year without success, why I didn't just give up. Why have I continued my own commitment to write, create, and pitch again and again? As if in response to this very question, the Ottawa International Animation Festival executive director, Chris Robinson, posted a message on CartoonBrew (*www.cartoonbrew.com*): "This obsession animators have with getting a TV series drives me crazy. Why is it your goal to have a TV series?" That's a good place to start this discussion. Why would one's goal be to have a TV series? Well, why would one have a goal to sell a painting, have a book published, win an Oscar, or run a film festival? A long-term goal helps to define a career's high point that goes far beyond our job-to-job existence. Is it crazy to want to make an impact or be recognized for excellence in one's field? Not everyone is suited for the goal of having his or her own TV series. In fact, as goals go, this one is a tall order, and as subjects go, this book has an enormous challenge: to realistically paint the process by which some creators have managed to dream up, pitch, sell, and make their cartoon series a reality within (or despite) the deeply flawed and imperfect world of development.

The Hard Truth

> "Pitching is so easy compared to actually running a show. If you can't handle the pitching process, the show will kill you."
> — Mo Willems, creator of *Sheep in the Big City* (Cartoon Network)

While this book won't shy away from the genuine frustrations associated with the would-be creator's point of view, it will not pander to them. A lot of creators behave as if just because they whipped a pitch book together they deserve to be rewarded with millions of dollars and a plum spot on the tube. These creators feel a sense of entitlement that puts them at war with those who ought to be their biggest allies: the development executives. As development executive Heather Kenyon tells it, "There can be this feeling of 'us vs. them,' or that we are 'just stupid executives.' There are some bad ones out there—I am not saying we are all angels. But frequently we are hard working people [who] are really trying to get the best shows on the air. We have a unique perspective on the network that can help the creator get their [*sic*] show picked up."

The sheer amount of raw anger spewing from some would-be creators helped convince me of the need of this book. Angry creators make several mistakes. For one, they undervalue the importance of relationships. Wouldn't selling your creation require you to work in partnership with a network development executive? Wouldn't they be the ones helping you navigate the corporate creative process, deadlines, Broadcast Standards & Practices, focus-group testing, and the needs of ancillary merchandise? Instead of feeling anger, maybe it's time to revisit those rejected pitches of yore. Trust me, this can be very enlightening. Of course, each and every time I pitched something, I was certain it was the best it could be. Often this translates into "the best I could do at the time." I now see many of my old projects in a new light. Often I discover that I wouldn't have greenlighted those pitches either! Happily, it's not all bad news. Through looking back, I am also able to take stock of how far I've come as a writer, creator, designer, and

My dad helped design this logo for my first animation pitch to secure a development deal. Thanks, Dad!

storyteller. Like a series of artist's sketchbooks, pitches also show the creator's development over time.

Along with the anger out there, there are scores of tales of why some animation artists or writers will never pitch shows again. Sometimes it takes only one negative event for them to talk themselves out of pitching forever. These are the animation development world's Miss Havishams. Broken-hearted and jilted to the core, they spread their gospel of "Why bother?" all over the Internet. In truth, most of these folks have a valid story to tell. I don't even mind their decisions to never pitch again, but that's like vowing never to walk again each time we stub a toe (*Never Walk Again* could make a snappy James Bond movie title). I suspect that if all it takes is one bad experience to convince you to stop chasing your dream, then that says more about your level of sincerity than it does about the flawed world of development.

I've chugged on, in part because pitching was never part of my plan for earning a living. I happen to earn my living happily toiling away in the animation industry. We animation artists wear many hats over the course of a typical career. In my career I've tackled character design, storyboards, layout, animation, and directing. Most importantly, I've made it a point to channel what I've learned into personal independent films. I find time spent on these films intoxicating. Here was a vehicle that let me play at being an animator, designer, writer, director, and producer long before anyone paid me commercially for those skills. In turn, the independent films served my career, eventually helping to land me my current job as a TV cartoon director of six series to date. Making time to write and develop pitch projects is something I do without having to depend on its success. Cartoon Network's *Codename: Kids Next Door* creator Tom Warburton agrees, saying, "Keep your day job. It never happens overnight."

The front of a postcard heralding my independent film *Good Morning*, a collaboration with composer Bob Charde. Independent films are exercises in total freedom, while at the same time offering commercial results. This film not only won awards at more than twelve festivals, but also led to two jobs and a continuing relationship with National Geographic Kids Entertainment.

In the world of development, slow and steady sometimes wins the race. While I spent ten years pitching without success, my otherwise blossoming career was busy enhancing my desirability as a creator. This is good news because, in reality, networks buy creators, not ideas. Heather Kenyon adds, "We are really looking for creators who are show runners; [people] who can take their experience and build a team that can put their vision on the screen. I suggest people get a job in the industry and start working their way up. Experience on every show comes into play when someone gets their own show. While working in the industry, you can learn how you want to run your show and maybe learn the things that other people did that you wouldn't want to repeat!"

Can you emerge from outside the industry and sell your show idea? The answer is yes, but in this scenario the creator usually fully executes his idea to a finished film, which might become tremendously popular after being posted online. This may get the attention of network executives seeking to parlay such success onto their channels. As this book will make perfectly clear, it would behoove both insiders and outsiders alike to start building relationships with others in their field. These can be creators, artists, writers, or directors they admire, as well as network development executives. Most of these folks are readily accessible. All you have to do is a little legwork while remembering to always be conscientious and respectful. You can meet such people at animation festivals and events or (in the virtual sense) by visiting animation sites online. Recently on AnimationNation.com (*www.AnimationNation.com*), one member asked if anyone knew a pitch contact at Disney's *Shorty McShorts' Shorts* development program. Moments later, the development executive himself answered the post and supplied his own contact info.

The Enemy Within

Of course, there is no guarantee we will ever sell anything. It is far easier to want your own show than it is to seriously work towards that goal, or to even be suited for that goal. As bad as our odds for success may be, the worst obstacle we face may be ourselves. The average reader of this book can probably benefit from years of practice writing scripts, making films, or working on someone else's show. For us to get anywhere in this book, we have to abandon the notion of expecting a network to let us develop our voices on its dime.

Developing as an artist and a writer is work, and work takes time. There are always a million reasons not to get started. For instance, a friend of mine had always wanted to finish a personal film. As the years passed, my friend always had a good reason not to get started. His first apartment was too hot. Then he moved, and his new apartment was too small. A third apartment did not have enough natural light. This story not only demonstrates that New Yorkers move a lot, but also shows how far one can go to keep oneself from one's goal. This may shock you, but I've never lived in a perfect apartment, either. In fact, my first apartment had bad light and a draft, and I didn't get along with my roommate. When it rained, water would cascade down my bedroom wall, soaking everything in its path. In my second apartment, the radiators sprayed water like an open hydrant. To this day, I can't look at a glass of water without cowering in fear. Yet somehow, these things did not stop me from making personal films, developing and pitching shows, and growing as an artist. I did those things because I sincerely wanted to achieve something. Of course, it wasn't always easy, and results often took years to materialize, but the important thing was that I was working toward my goals nearly every day. When you're in your old age, looking back at your career, will you be able to say that you went after your dream?

Clearing the Mystery

There are no real mysteries in this business. Things only seem so when we don't yet have the answer. Mystery is supposed to be a temporary thing, not a permanent condition—well, unless you're Agatha Christie. Seriously, a primary goal of this book is to clear up whatever questions you may have about the pitching and development process, such as:

- How to tap into your creativity to develop something personal, yet universal

- How to improve your project through collaborations and partnerships

- How to hone your ideas into a perfect pitch package

- How to set up pitch meetings

- How and when to get legal representation and agents

- How to manage the emotional roller coaster common to the pitching and development process

- How a greenlight unfolds, from a development deal, to a pilot, to a series

- How creators and development executives collaborate and define their roles on a project

- How to create a dream production, not only for you, but also for your collaborators and crew

The Seemingly Changing World of Development

When I wrote my first book, *Your Career in Animation: How to Survive and Thrive*, I was very conscious that it would be a mistake to feature any content that might date the book. Instead, my focus was to create a guide that might help one learn the importance of reputation and relationships to any healthy career in animation. This new book might seem like it's rooted in the present in its depiction of a world of TV development executives, with television as the dominate means of program delivery. I'm not concerned with this problem dating this book in the least. No matter how the paradigm shifts away from conventional television to broadband Internet channels, iPods, cell phones, and wristwatches, these are merely technological changes. If anything, these new platforms will create an even greater need for creator-driven content. At the end of the day, it will still be the big media companies and networks in control of the new TV model.

It is also extremely naïve to assume that creators acting alone without the need of a bigger distribution will be the models of the future. Right now it only seems so because of our freedom to post our own creations on personal Web sites or at free destinations such as YouTube. At the time of this writing, recent graduate Alex Butera had been offered a development deal by a Web destination after his student film, *Baman Piderman*, was a featured video on YouTube. While such Web sites may help you get discovered, the resulting development deals offered by a network or broadband channel follow the traditional model of TV development or something quite similar. I can't imagine a time when creators will not be pitching to big companies in some form or another. Anytime a creator seeks to gain funding or distribution for a project, a pitch will be involved. I think this ensures that this book will remain a useful resource. It's been said before: the more things change, the more they stay the same.

Lightning in a Bottle

> "I've had pitches that went terribly and ended up in series being produced. Alternatively, I've had pitches that rocked their world and went nowhere. Either they want you or they don't."
> —**Mo Willems, creator of *Sheep in the Big City* (Cartoon Network)**

In terms of odds, pitching a show is similar to trying to win the state lottery. But perhaps a better example would be to compare our odds for success against the chances of being struck by lightning. No one knows exactly where or when lightning may strike, but one can certainly increase the likelihood of being struck by chasing a thunderstorm and flying a kite with a key tied to its string. In a strange but similar way, this book will attempt to better your odds for a direct hit. I hope you don't mind getting a little crispy.

Chapter 1

Beginnings

> "The pitching system is a bad system, though it works for a lot of people. . . . I see many talented artists working very hard pitching shows all the time. If they funneled that kind of energy toward making a film, they might have a little something more to show for it."
>
> —Patrick Smith, independent animator (excerpt from an interview published on AWN.com)

I didn't plan to open this book with a quote like the one above, yet for this book to be of any use, we have to tackle all opinions, attitudes, myths, and unrealistic expectations that can cloud the reality of creating, pitching, and selling an animated series. Emerging after time spent staffing TV shows such *Doug, Daria*, and *Downtown*, Patrick Smith successfully transitioned to become the owner/operator of his own boutique-style animation studio in New York City. Out of his TriBeCa headquarters, Smith splits his time among making award-winning world-class festival films, teaching, and working away on his real bread and butter: commercials.

A good place to begin our subject is right back at Patrick Smith's quote. (Take a moment to reread it—I'll sit right here whistling *The Girl from Ipanema* until you return.) Smith gives us a great starting place because he's really speaking about where a would-be creator might best spend her creative time and energy: making independent films and projects or pitching to TV networks, Web destinations, etc. While it's an important question, it doesn't sound like a question anyone could answer for someone else.

A still from Patrick Smith's award-winning film, *Puppet*. Image courtesy of the artist.

In the independent films model, creators (working over a period of years or even a lifetime) have the opportunity to nurture their creative sensibilities via their art: independent films. Independent films are free of network tampering, the fickleness of fads, and the potentially lethal power of focus-group testing or bad ratings. Independent animator Breehn Burns summed it up well in a quote from my last book: "Pitches and pilots amounted to hours and months and years of my work sitting on some executive's desk somewhere with a sticky note on top reading, 'maybe.' So instead of making pitches I make short films."

Fair enough, but does time spent making independent films best prepare a creator for creating, developing, and selling an idea to any given network that caters to a specialized segment of the viewing audience? Seems to me the answer would have a lot to do with the type of independent films the creator is drawn to make. For pure artistic and nuts-and-bolts filmic knowledge, little can beat the creative laboratory of making your own personal films. To do so is an exercise in total freedom, limited only by your time, imagination, talent, and available resources. These films make great breeding grounds for your voice as a director and a storyteller. Independent films run the gamut, from experimental works à la Oscar Fischinger to the more entertainment-based shorts of Bill Plympton and Don Hertzfeldt.

In the latter category, it would be hard to imagine two filmmakers more at home right where they are; these two are masters of one-shot humorous films that draw their creative mojo from concepts or situations as opposed to those inspired by or from character. Interestingly enough, animation artists making independent films are more often better prepared for directing animated TV commercials than for helming their own series. Although it may seem like the words "independent" and "commercial" don't go together, in this case, they happily do. Great indie films are often short and graphically pleasing. Is it any wonder that these films would attract the attention of Madison Avenue? One merely has to look at Ron Diamond's stable of Acme Filmworks commercial directors to see that most of them are top indie filmmakers such as Patrick Smith, Bill Plympton, Wendy Tilby, Amanda Forbis, Joanna Quinn, Paul Driessen, Chris Hinton, Janet Perlman, Frank and Caroline Mouriss, and Michael Duduk Dewitt (among many, many others).

However, there have also been independent filmmakers such as Matt Stone and Trey Parker (*South Park*), and Mike Judge (*Beavis & Butt-Head*) whose indie creations are entertaining short films that derive their own

The Uncomfortable Circle

KILL EVERY BODY

©Xeth•com

"Luckily, the most recent studies on potential harmful effects of video games are largely inconclusive."

A sample of Xeth Feinberg's online comic strip *The Uncomfortable Circle*, which displays the same signature wit as his animation work. Image courtesy of the artist.

quirky brand of comedy out of their idiosyncratic characters, creating a veritable series-sized bonanza of possibilities. We could ask ourselves why the creators of these top shows did not get pulled into the world of directing TV commercials. Why, instead, were they so suited for success in the world of series TV? The answer is, in part, a creator's affinity and interest in characters. Development executive Peter Gal explains, "A character should be funny even if left alone in their room for two minutes." I'd venture that the aforementioned two shows pass that test with flying colors.

In terms of writing preparation for a would-be creator, any serial-style storytelling is good training. Comic strips, graphic novels, comics, and Web toons with recurring characters can give you the understanding of which ideas can sustain such episodic adventures and the strength that is necessary of characters in order for them to go that distance.

Successfully creating, selling, and producing your animated series requires a specific balance of skills, which will likely require years to develop. According to Mo Willems, you should make films both by yourself and with a crew under you. "Both forms of filmmaking are essential to the constraints of a big production. Essentially, you need enough experience to be able to do every job on your production and the wisdom to have hired people that are better than you at each of those jobs," says Willems.

Creative Inspiration

It all starts with an idea. Many creators draw upon their childhoods for inspiration. Like with all good writing, you want to inject a kernel of truth that can only come from personal experience. David Fine, co-creator of *Bob and Margaret* (Snowden Fine Productions and Nelvana Limited) channeled personal experiences such as feelings about aging, thoughts on friendship, and issues he and his wife were dealing with, like whether or not to have children. Other times, a creative way to begin might be to imagine a concept that the intended audience can relate to. A writing partner and I created a pitch called *Teddy and Annie*, which focused on the two weird kids on the block. It was a good theme, familiar and relatable to most any child. We also mixed things up by using historical figures as a launching point to write the characters. Teddy was based on Teddy Roosevelt, a childhood hero of mine, and Annie was based on Annie Oakley, another larger-than-life figure out of our nation's past. Once you have some jumping-off points, you can build from there to create and

Jim Jinkins's series *Pinky Dinky Doo* was inspired by the creator's family interactions. Copyright 2008, Cartoon Pizza and Sesame Workshop.

develop memorable characters. Remember that even Homer Simpson started out aping the antics and voice of actor Walter Matthau before coming into his own yellow skin.

Other creators develop stories by performing non-linear thinking exercises (like pulling words out of a hat and writing a situation inspired by the word). This is one method favored by Stephen Hillenburg, creator of *SpongeBob SquarePants* (Nickelodeon). Hillenburg says, "Ultimately the ideas that stick are the ones that consistently make everyone laugh." There's no one set magic formula to creating winning characters. Sometimes, even a trip to the museum could prove inspiring in unforeseen ways. Hillenburg shares, "I was at this museum once that had a room full of cartoony Mike Kelley drawings that were all really bizarre. A group of elementary kids led by a museum docent entered the room and got really excited about the drawings. A few were examining this depiction of, I think, Abe Lincoln with brain waves and others were pointing at this one drawing of a goose biting a little boy on the penis. The docent was clearly uncomfortable and quickly ushered them out of the room (against their will) to the next exhibit. I've always wanted *SpongeBob* to be that compelling." Of course, a great deal of the inspiration for Hillenburg's series came from his interest in marine biology and surf culture.

Even the ordinary moments of daily life may serve to inspire a creator. Jim Jinkins, creator of *Doug* as well as the recent series *Pinky Dinky Doo*, reports that ideas for his series come from daydreams and doodles during boring business meetings, from bedtime stories he makes up for his two kids, and from simply watching people. *Blue's Clues* co-creator Traci Paige Johnson channeled her love of *Schoolhouse Rock* and *Sesame Street* animations and other influences to help her dream up the art style for *Blue's Clues*: "My love of Fruit Stripe Gum became Steve's shirt and my love of the categorized colors in an art store became the color scheme of Blue's house." Jackson Publick, creator of Adult Swim's *The Venture Bros.* on Cartoon Network, was initially inspired by a vague-but-powerful memory of *Jonny Quest* cartoons he saw as a kid and exposure to old Tom Swift novels through an older friend. Four seasons later, Publick's series remains faithful to its original inspiration while, at the same time, having expanded its scope to develop its own voice.

Cracking the Code

"It's all about character, stupid!" This is a good (albeit rude) slogan, but how does this break down when it comes to developing characters in an animated idea? A quick survey of the top animated series cartoons since 1991 reveals that most have at least one aspect in common: a simple twist upon our expectations. *The Powerpuff Girls* are three preschoolers who happen to have been burdened with the larger-than-life responsibility of saving the day before bedtime. *Johnny Bravo* is a self-declared ladies' man who can't get a date. Jenny XG79 (*My Life as a Teenage Robot*) is a teenager whose adolescence is complicated by the fact that she happens to be a robot. *Courage the Cowardly Dog* is actually a scaredy-cat who is forced time and time again into bravery against his own nature. *Juniper Lee, Avatar,* and *Danny Phantom* are preteens who happen to be "chosen" to fight some kind of evil, making their lives complicated and so much cooler (in a Buffy Summers sort of way).

Sensing a pattern yet? A twist on the norm as your premise is a good place to start developing character because the twist leads to natural opportunities for conflict, which, in turn, reveals character. How do the above characters deal with their problems? Do they have a sense of humor about them? Are they defensive? Are they insecure? How does this affect their interaction with others? With some thought, the character's conflicts become the engine for hundreds of episodes worth of stories.

One thing is for certain: to draw inspiration from the characters listed above would be a very poor beginning. That would be akin to copying a copy of a copy. Remember, Bugs Bunny is already a copy of Groucho Marx. The best bet is to draw experience from real life, or if that fails, from living persons in history, TV, film, literature, and theater. *The Ren & Stimpy Show* creator John Kricfalusi likes to cite Carroll O'Connor's performance as Archie Bunker in *All in the Family* as an ultimate example of "character." I appreciate the example, but my gold standard for character is Peter Falk's portrayal of TV's Lt. Columbo. In this role, Falk has it all. On the surface, Columbo is scruffy, unfocused, unprepared, and forgetful. In this way, murderers don't see him as much of a threat, and often even attempt to "help" him solve the case by trying to steer him to false conclusions. Often it is far too late before they realize that the bumbling lieutenant is actually a genius investigator with a sharp, curious, and agile mind.

Peter Falk brings a lot of human likability to the part, and we get ample opportunity to get to know the real Columbo through information he shares about his wife and also through other glimpses into his personal life, such as his relationship with his dog. On top of everything, Columbo is also a very distinct-looking character, with his cockeyed stare, rumpled raincoat, bedhead, five o'clock shadow, and ever-present cigar. We identify with Columbo not only because of his abilities as a detective, but also because he is a fish out of water, a slob investigating murders in high society. He's the "every man," and each victory he scores is a win for our side. It's quite an ingenious combination of factors and is no doubt part of why Columbo is one of television's most beloved characters, having survived for decades on a notoriously fickle tube.

Creative Obstacles

Another breed of would-be creators hatch their brilliant ideas for cartoon series when they are nine years old. They cling to their moldy ideas like life rafts, enabling them to shut off any other creative thought that might otherwise pop into their heads. After all, why bother to keep writing,

Character show art created for the author's pitch *There's Something About Gregory*, co-created with Debbie Staab and developed by Allan Neuwirth. The character poses, drawn by artist Matt Peters, show a range of expression and attitudes, revealing this character's personality based on art alone. Image courtesy of the author.

creating, and developing, when you reached perfection in pre-adolescence? It's a given that most successful creators have been creating since a very young age. The problem occurs when creators freeze-dry their talents in childhood, and spend their adulthoods scheming on how best to exploit the fruits of their youth. This is a mistake on many levels. First off, who among us is the same person he was at a young age? Our creations represent where we are emotionally and mentally during that particular point in our career. Creative development happens hand in hand with growing maturity and life experiences. Nobody is suggesting you have to jettison your past—in fact, a good balance, especially when creating for children, would be to retain a bridge to your childhood experience—but it should be a source of inspiration, not the summation of it.

A series, by nature, requires lots and lots of additional ideas. If you manage to sell your freeze-dried idea, you will likely have a very hard time expanding upon it. Creative writing and development are not things you can turn on after decades of inactivity. One needs to keep one's mind sharp. Continuing to develop new ideas over a period of time gives one room to stretch her creativity and to feed the beast should her creations happen to sell.

The next self-inflicted detriment to creativity is what I call "getting stuck." Getting stuck is staying in one phase of writing and development for years or decades at a time. One example is a friend of mine who has been researching her idea for over six years now. She is constantly studying the historic period in which her project is set. She's read dozens of books on the subject, taken pads of notes, and even traveled to historic locations. As much as I admire her dedication, I'm worried that she's stuck in the research stage. Perhaps the answer, for her, would be to take on a collaborator who could absorb all the great research and funnel it into a pitchable format. Bringing in such help requires a creator to let go of some control. Happily, letting go of control is a good thing. It prepares one for the collaborative process that is making a series. Despite changing technology, there is no such thing as a series made by an individual. As in any field, the challenge of working well with others is often harder than doing the work itself. A little practice will help prepare you to helm a show one day.

There are lots of other ways to get stuck, too. On a development panel at the first-ever Platform International Animation Festival, a young woman in the audience asked a question. She said that she had spent a ton of time designing two great characters that she claimed to know inside and out. Her only problem was difficulty writing stories that utilized those characters. Development executive Heather Kenyon helpfully answered, "My first thought is that if you're having trouble putting your characters in situations, your characters are probably not as well-developed as you think." Here was a case of a creator stuck in the design phase, believing that to design a character is to create a character. For a character to become fully realized, you have to write the character as well as design it. Not only should a character have conflicts (both internal and external), it must also be interesting to watch while eating a ham sandwich.

Some creators get stuck not being able to simplify their pitch into bite-sized elements for easy saleability. Other creators get stuck because they don't know how to meet and pitch to executives. To keep parts of the process a mystery is the same as making excuses. Only you can decide whether being stuck is a temporary setback or evidence of weeding yourself out of the game. I would venture that being stuck is a way of keeping mystery in the process of writing, creating, and pitching, which is a form of self-sabotage. It is this book's goal to shed light on those dark spots, explaining how today's top creators developed, organized, pitched, and produced their projects. My hope is that this will empower and inspire the reader to pursue her dream with confidence.

How Young is Too Young?

The entertainment industry is a business of youth, but does a creator need to be a certain age before they seriously start pitching? When I was a student at the School of Visual Arts, Hanna-Barbera announced a storyboard contest that aggressively reached out to kids and teen creators. Years later I had the pleasure of interviewing one of those contest winners, Alex Kirwan, for my first book. Kirwan was truly an incredible artist right out of the gate. After winning the storyboard contest, he began his career in animation fresh out of high school. His first job in the business was creating a few original shorts for Frederator's *Oh Yeah! Cartoons* anthology for Nickelodeon. In 2006, at the Los Angeles launch of my book, *Your Career in Animation: How to Survive and Thrive*, Alex Kirwan was one of my panelists and I was delighted to make his acquaintance in person. On the panel, he openly reflected on those formative years making his films for *Oh Yeah! Cartoons*: "Back then I believed that I could be a creator of shorts for a living. I was in for a shock when my next pitch idea wasn't picked up and Frederator executive, Eric Homan, advised me to take a job on someone else's series and begin again from bottom up."

Kirwan took that advice, perhaps out of necessity more than anything else. He restarted his career working as a prop designer and climbed up the ranks to become one of the top art directors/designers working in animation today, showcasing his mature style on such projects as Rob Renzetti's *My Life as a Teenage Robot* (Nickelodeon/Frederator). Certainly, when Kirwan chooses to re-enter the pitching arena he will not be the same creator he was twelve years ago. He'll carry with him years of seasoned experience working for others in this most collaborative of the arts.

Since Kirwan's career began, there are now more homegrown would-be creators out there than ever. Affordable and user-friendly animation software, such as Adobe's AfterEffects and Flash, has unleashed these living room Hanna-Barberas on an unsuspecting nation. As president of ASIFA-East, I've seen a new wave of young filmmakers making their presence known while still in high school. This generation, frequent portfolio bloggers and festival attendees, is growing up creatively in public perhaps as never before in this industry's history. But should they be pitching at

An Alex Kirwan–designed character rotation from Cartoon Network's *Time Squad*. *Time Squad*, its logo, and all related characters and elements are trademarks of and © 2008 The Cartoon Network.

such a young age? I say, Why not? Most often, to create a meaningful piece of art, one should have lived a little. At age eleven, we are not the same people we may become by age twenty-one. For one thing, our clothes fit very differently.

One could argue that the younger a creator is, the better, especially if they're pitching animation for children. The idea is, the closer a creator is to their intended audience, the better suited he is to write for that audience. I challenge this notion. Sure, with regard to age, young creators are closest to their audience. The problem is that most young creators have nothing to say. They have nothing to compare their experiences to, no context in which to find a larger meaning. Today's budding pitchers would be wise to follow the second leg of Kirwan's career, in which he started over, paid his dues in the studio system, and developed the long-term chops that have served his career well to this day.

Still not convinced? When I was a child, I hated coffee and onions. Now, scarcely a day goes by when I don't enjoy both—though not usually at the same time, mind you. And while my breath may be worse for the wear, this certainly shows how our tastes change with age. We're supposed to grow as people, and in our case, as writers and artists. I'm grateful for my years on this earth and what my experiences have taught me. All the stumbles, lessons, and triumphs I've encountered along the way inform my creations.

Chapter 2

Preparing a Pitch Part I: The Two-Sheet

> "The main mistake I've made is not being thorough enough. Not having every single question answered. That's a big no-no. Always have as many answers about your project as possible."
>
> —**Butch Hartman, creator of *The Fairly OddParents* and *Danny Phantom* (Nickelodeon)**

What do you have to do to sell an animated series pitch? Gosh, if we could answer that with one definitive answer for every creator and every project, there probably wouldn't be a need for this book. That would mean I'd have a lot more free time this year and a lot fewer trees would have had to sacrifice their pulpy, paper-making goodness. Unfortunately, there is no single universal answer to this question. However, we can assume that a well-connected and established creator has less to prove than a newcomer or a relative unknown to the industry. An easy formula here is the less grand your reputation, the more heavy lifting you'll be expected to do in the pitch process.

Recently, there was a major backlash on CartoonBrew.com when it was leaked that the creator of a new animated show got picked up straight for a series because the creator simply told his pal (who happened to be a top network president) that he wanted to do a series about music or

A still from an episode I directed of Cartoon Network's Adult Swim series, *Assy McGee*. This unconventional series has a surprising amount of spontaneity, depth, and character development. And I'm not just kissing ass here. *Assy McGee*, its logo, and all related characters and elements are trademarks of and © 2008 The Cartoon Network.

something. Thus a series was signed, sealed, and soon delivered, completely bypassing the rigorous development track that other creators are left to navigate. On the bright side, the multi-season series order created employment for a lot of people. Development stories like this one are not reasons to give up. It would be naïve to think that all projects are carefully selected by merit and that all creators are welcomed equally.

In another example, Cartoon Network's Adult Swim series *Assy McGee* was greenlighted after its co-creator, Carl W. Adams, showed a one-minute test film of the project to Mike Lazzo (senior executive vice president in charge of Adult Swim). "Great. Give us twenty of these," was Lazzo's response. Adams was temporarily dumbstruck. He had neither bible nor concrete plan for additional episodes. The strength of the test film and Adam's ample experience as a key creative on such series as Cartoon Network's *Home Movies* were enough to warrant a pick up. Subsequently, *Assy McGee* proved itself to be worthy of a series, quickly earning a cult following and a high-profile sponsor, and eventually employing this author as animation director.

Still from Fran Krause's RISD thesis film, *Mr. Smile* (1999), which not only scored success at film festivals around the globe, but also led to three development deals and two pilots at Cartoon Network. Is it too late for me to enroll at RISD? Image courtesy of the artist.

There are lots of nontraditional success stories out there. One that comes to mind is how Fran Krause's killer Rhode Island School of Design student film, *Mr. Smile,* caught the attention of then–Cartoon Network development executive Linda Simensky. The two first met at an animation festival in Sweden, and soon Fran was invited to pitch to Cartoon Network. At the time, I was working with Fran on *Blue's Clues* (Nick, Jr.). I'll never forget the day that Fran told us he'd be leaving to make his own pilot, with co-creator Will Krause, for Cartoon Network. He was not even a year out of school! In Fran's development story, his student film became his most important pitch element, helping to pave the way for his early pitching success. Subsequently, Fran and Will Krause went on to score two more development deals with Cartoon Network over the next five years, culminating in a second pilot, which may lead to a series.

The three success stories show the importance of building reputations and forging relationships, which factor into every development success story I can think of. Reputation and relationships are intertwined because both come from one's work history: the projects one has worked on, one's role on those projects, and how effectively one built and preserved healthy relationships with others in the industry.

Whatever reputations and relationships we have, it is important that we be able to organize and convey the ideas we pitch in the most precise manner possible. Since the basic rule of measure in animation development is the pitch "bible," it is here that our challenge begins.

The Two-Sheet

However, before we open up the Pandora's box of the pitch bible, we need to cozy up to the pitch bible's lean and scrappy cousin, the two-sheet. No, not two-ply toilet paper, although we all appreciate its softness, durability, and perforated edge. The two-sheet, for our purposes, is really a first step mini-pitch bible that contains a one-sentence series log line, some show art, very brief descriptions of the world and its rules, character descriptions, and sample plot lines.

The two-sheet is a teaser, an important first step before going further with your idea. The two-sheet makes a great starting point for beginners and established professionals alike. The first advantage is that the two-sheet is a low-risk way to present your idea because it's quick and inexpensive to create. This means that it may be possible to bring, perhaps, three individual ideas to a pitch meeting. The world of development is a fickle place. Each network has its own ever-changing needs. The two-sheet gives the creator an opportunity to throw three ideas against the wall and see what may stick. At the very least, a two-sheet starts the conversation. One of the most inspiring bits of pitching information I've heard is that all *SpongeBob SquarePants* creator Stephen Hillenburg was trying to accomplish with his first pitch meeting was to interest Nickelodeon in a second meeting. A two-sheet pitch proposal might just be the document that starts you on your way.

Most development executives are open to seeing your idea evolve over time and over the course of several meetings. Development executive Peter Gal affirms, "I am definitely open to looking at pitches again. Hopefully, the creator resubmitting the pitch has really taken our thoughts to heart and [has] made some real changes." Out of all my pitching adventures, I've only encountered three times when development executives did not welcome seeing a re-pitch of a past proposal. In the most frustrating of all cases, I had pitched to a former top network executive who is now president of his own successful independent production company. In the meeting, I pitched four or five ideas, only one of which received some interest. Near the end of the meeting, the president asked, "What else ya got?" I told him about a project that was in its earliest stages. I happened to have a pencil sketch of the idea on me. He encouraged me to show it, however raw it might be. He seemed to like the idea and expressed an openness to seeing it again.

Months later I returned to his company to properly pitch the previously underdeveloped idea along with another proposal. The president did not have time to take the meeting this time so I pitched to his second-in-command and her assistant. Both ideas seemed to generate a lot of enthusiasm. The meeting stretched to almost two hours, which was very encouraging. Imagine my surprise when the assistant rang me up a few weeks later to say that they had not shown the redeveloped old idea to the president because he had already passed on it. In their eyes, he had seen that idea, albeit in embryonic form, so he didn't need to see it again. It was a pass. Dead on arrival. My willingness to show a work in progress had probably done me in. The lesson is that an idea isn't ready to pitch until it is at least in the form of a two-sheet proposal.

Another advantage to the two-sheet is that you'll be more likely to receive quicker and more honest feedback during the pitch meeting. A pitch meeting featuring a many-paged pitch bible is often harder for development executives to digest. They will likely feel compelled to hold off on giving too much feedback until they've had a chance to read the whole document, and that can take a very long time. Executives can tell when a creator has spent a lot of time and energy putting together a pitch bible, and sometimes this might make them reluctant to give honest or prompt feedback. Development executive Heather Kenyon adds, "I just feel worse telling [the artist] we are passing since [the artist has] taken all this time." This doesn't mean that it's a bad idea to spend lots of time and energy on a pitch, but it does demonstrate that one might be better off first pitching with a simpler and more concise two-sheet.

Not surprisingly, seasoned industry professionals with pre-established reputations are the most sought after or desired creators. Sometimes veteran creators even score a greenlight based on a two-sheet proposal. This makes sense, although I've seen this logic carried way beyond reason. During a meeting with two young executives of one network's shorts development program, I learned what they expected to see in a pitch. After

Contact info:
David B. Levy
~~22 50 32nd Avenue #22~~
~~Astoria, NY 11105~~
~~646-331-9592~~
~~david.levy@nick.com~~

"Hard To Swallow"

A series proposal created by David B. Levy and Dale Clowdis
Rough Draft treatment
7/10/01

The story of three childhood buddies, a worm named **Osmond**, a cat named **Smudge** and a mockingbird named **Scout** who live in the same backyard. All three are struggling to retain their friendship into their adolescence. The challenge is that as they mature, their natural instincts are kicking in which make them want to eat each other up. Can they survive their friendship? Can they survive each other? Do you find this concept, "**Hard to Swallow**?" If not, read on:

Osmond is an insecure worm that over compensates by habitually making bad puns. Inadvertently, this tendency has served another purpose because whenever Scout has the urge to devour Osmond, his bad puns make her lose her appetite. Osmond's insecurity is largely based on him not knowing his own gender or that of his parents. Osmond has never been seen outside of his apple. The apple is Osmond's pseudo-body (he even wears a T-shirt over it to complete the effect). It also acts as his security blanket, also providing nourishment, and sanctuary. Not surprisingly, Osmond has earned the nickname "Granny Smith". Osmond is forever jealous of what he perceives to be the perfect families and home-life of his two friends. Osmond's parents are dirt farmers who live in a hole in the yard. They are always quick to offer Osmond quaint home-spun advice that often ends up taking on surprising relevance to the three young friends.

Scout Mockingbird is over-confident and bossy and outwardly tries to mold her friends in her own image. Inwardly, she is glad that Osmond and Smudge are dependent on her leadership qualities and hopes to keep it that way. In her birdhouse, Scout has taken on a larger role since the disappearance of her mother and is now accustomed to having more adult responsibilities and freedoms. Scout's mother mysteriously vanished some time ago...and is believed to be deceased at the paws of Smudge's dad, Mr. Catlick. This touchy subject often bursts out of Scout at inappropriate times, much to the embarrassment of Smudge. Scout's father, Atticus Mockingbird, is a moral, kindly and mellow bird. Scout constantly sabotages any chance Atticus has of meeting somebody new that might result in her having to share his affections. Although Scout is over-bearing, Atticus is more than a match for her because he has a way of gently manipulating her into minding him without her knowing it.

Page one of the initial two-sheet for *Hard to Swallow,* my pitch with Dale Clowdis. Note the series synopsis and character descriptions. While this proved enough to interest Cartoon Network in seeing more, the lackluster artwork and overall dull presentation in this two-sheet couldn't have helped our case. One should make a two-sheet as fun a document as possible so that it may best reflect the tone of the show being pitched.

Smudge Catlick and his family occupy the old shed in the yard. The Catlick's have an unspecified huge number of offspring. Smudge is constantly meeting new siblings that he had no idea existed. Not surprisingly, Smudge sees himself as a number and not an individual. Because Smudge does not receive enough attention at home, he has never had positive or negative reinforcement...nor has he learned any of the basics of life. Smudge only knows his parents as the fighting and arguing silhouettes in the shed window. To Scout, Smudge is the ultimate ball of clay to be molded into anything she sees fit. Their friendship is a tenuous one, because at any given time Smudge's uncontrollable instincts kick in and he pounces on her with murderous intent. After these moments of terror, Smudge blacks out and wakes up with no memory of the incidents.

Sample Plot Lines

-Osmond discovers another worm living in his apple that his friends and family end up liking more than him.
-When a new singles community for birds moves in nearby, Scout is desperate to stop her father from meeting someone.
-After Scout returns from a two week trip, she becomes the object of Smudge's affections, as he believes that she has become a "woman". Meanwhile, all this gender specific business has Osmond confused.
-The friends' parents pass hostile messages to each other through their children.
-After witnessing two wildlife deaths in the yard, the friends, believing that death comes in threes, go into hiding.
- Scout tries to prove why its best to live in a nest up a tree....inadvertently making Osmond, a worm, into a sitting duck for birds.
-Mr. Catlick holds Osmond hostage for his amusement as his own personal play thing.
-Scout invites Osmond over to dinner and eats worms in his presence for the first time.
-Osmond and Scout bond when they both feel left out while others are celebrating Mother's Day.

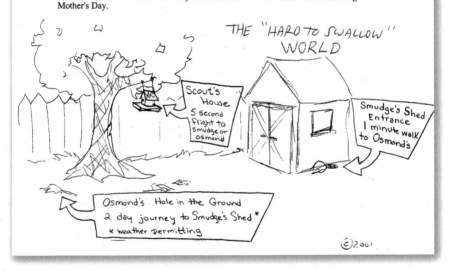

The second page of the *Hard to Swallow* two-sheet pitch. It was a mistake to try to depict each sample plot in one sentence, even in a format as abbreviated as a two-sheet. The layout of the world is clear, but it's not unique or indicative of a creator's point of view. Every element, whether written or drawn, should appear as if it could have only come from the creator's vision.

presenting a mini-bible for my idea, I was told I had done way too much work. When I asked them how much work they were used to seeing, the answer came back, "nothing." Well, I had done considerably more than nothing. Then they walked me through several of their completed shorts as well as others they had in development. I asked what those creators had shown to score their deals. "Nothing," was again the answer.

Sporting a bubble pipe and Sherlock Holmes cap, I investigated more deeply. It turns out that all of the creators were big names with oodles of experience on top projects. One was a former Pixar art director. Another was a star from the comics world. A third had already helmed a series for another network. Apparently, in each case, all the prospective creator had had to do was provide a one-sentence sound bite, something like: "I want to do a cartoon spoofing *American Idol*." Score! Instant greenlight! I soon learned that this shorts program catered to fads and that most of its shorts were based on fleeting pop culture. I'll be very surprised if the next hit animated series evolves out of such a shallow and creatively disposable development program.

Good and bad development scenarios aside, the two-sheet is a creator's best friend. Two-sheets are easy to create, may help you get more instant and honest feedback during a pitch meeting, and could help generate interest for another meeting. In any event, a two-sheet is a natural place to start before digging into the far more complex, more time-consuming, and meatier document known as a pitch bible.

When Is Enough Enough?

> "You will be pitching your idea to people who have millions of dollars to spend on someone, and they need to feel confident about where they spend it. If you come into the meeting not having any clue as to what your project is or where its potential is, then they won't either."
>
> —**Butch Hartman, creator of *The Fairly OddParents* and *Danny Phantom*** **(Nickelodeon)**

In ten years, I pitched about ten projects and never hit a home run. Looking back over the bones of all these projects, I can see one common denominator: I always placed limitations on how much work I was willing to do. I was so in love with each proposal that I truly believed that even the minimal amount of effort would be enough to convince others to agree. For each of these pitches, I often created only one piece of show art, a sample script, and a two-sheet. The artwork was slick enough, but the characters were usually depicted in a void, not interacting with their world or each other.

The two-sheet contained short blurbs describing characters, the set-up or world, and a few sentences for each plot idea. With such slim pickins, even development executives who wanted to work with me (and saw potential in my ideas) didn't have enough strong material to help shepherd my projects up the development ladder. I know now that I hadn't done enough work to seal a deal, and it's a mind-bender to imagine how many great opportunities may have slipped through my fingers.

Again, there's no single easy answer to how much work you need to do to sell your cartoon pitch. Some creators have to do next to no work while others produce entire test films to snag their greenlights. A recent experience with former development executive Alex Manugian at Cartoon Network helped me finally crack the code of how much is enough.

In the fall of 2006, I flew to Los Angeles to launch my first book at an event sponsored by ASIFA Hollywood. While on the coast, I snuck in a meeting with then–Cartoon Network development executives Heather Kenyon and Alex Manugian and pitched a new project co-created with Debbie Staab and developed by Allan Neuwirth. Although a deal did not materialize from it, the pitch meeting went great, and afterwards Manugian took me to lunch where we had fun connecting on an informal, personal level over some juicy burgers. Several months later, he called and told me that Cartoon Network development executives had agonized over whether to option our pitch. "You are in the top 5 percent of what we're considering," Manugian added. Following this, he gave me a short list of notes and suggestions to help our project get ready for an option. Their notes made sense to my team and me, and we were excited to incorporate them.

I asked Manugian what our project was missing that, despite their enthusiasm, would not enable them to option it at this time. I knew this was a tough question to throw out there, but I believed that the answer could help my collaborators and me to seal the deal on the next try. He answered, "Right now you are on the cusp of convincing us to option this, but we need to be completely convinced." Although seemingly vague, Manugian's answer was the key to development in a nutshell. As creators pitching, we aren't asking for much. We simply want companies or networks to spend millions of dollars in blind faith that our daydreams might turn out to be the next *SpongeBob SquarePants*. Okay, maybe we are asking for a lot! Is it any wonder that we need to fully convince networks beyond a shadow of a doubt before they are ready to start handing over bags of money with dollar signs on them?

The two-sheet is not meant to be the document that fully convinces a network or company to greenlight a project, although it is possible that it could be. Most often, the two-sheet is a useful first salvo in the pitching process, demonstrating the potential of a creator's voice and vision and helping to test the collaborative waters between network and creator. The creator's next challenge is to expand and demonstrate that vision, sewing it up tightly into a four- to eight-page booklet that often does its hardest work long after you've left the room. Cue the dramatic music as we segue into the next chapter.

Chapter 3

Preparing a Pitch Part II: The Pitch Bible

"I think the most important elements to have in a pitch bible are who the characters are: What do they want; What are their flaws; How do they relate to each other; [and] What world do they inhabit. But all of this should be in an easily digestible format. Simple and sweet. Get to the point. Illustrate the ideas with a few drawings. If you have these elements, it should be easy to see stories that could happen. A common mistake is blocks of endless text. If it's not quickly scannable, it probably won't be read."

—**Carl H. Greenblatt, creator of** *Chowder* **(Cartoon Network)**

There was an interesting discussion concerning pitch bibles at an ASIFA-East event celebrating Frederator's launch of the Nickelodeon shorts anthology series *Random! Cartoons*. I served as the moderator of a panel, which included Frederator president and executive producer, Fred Seibert, and several creators of his shorts. I introduced the topic of pitching in storyboards versus the traditional pitch bible. The method of choice for Frederator is that would-be creators pitch their ideas in a storyboard form that is essentially the film before a film is made. The characters are shown in action, activated by a plot, which hopefully springs out of the

A promotional image of Carl H. Greenblatt's *Chowder*, showing the character having a real gas of a time. *Chowder*, its logo, and all related characters and elements are trademarks of and © 2008 The Cartoon Network.

characters themselves. This method is very direct and I can see why it appeals to Frederator, which (with its order of thirty-nine cartoons) was in the business of making shorts, not series. Frederator creator Manny Galan adds, "Frederator was the first company that didn't want any of that stereotypical pitch book stuff. They wanted a storyboard depicting an entire seven-minute story. Unconventional and overwhelming, but smart and effective. Nothing will sell your cartoon better than an actual board depicting your cartoon."

True enough words for development at Frederator, but the fact remains that the pitch bible is the pitch document of choice just about everywhere else. A good pitch bible contains lots of splashy show art (eye candy); succinct, fun-to-read descriptions of the characters, the world, and the rules of the world; and some episode synopses. I created a half-dozen storyboard pitches during a year of pitching and re-pitching to Frederator. It was a very rewarding experience creatively but, ultimately, storyboards alone are just not very useful tools when pitching anywhere else. Only after I scrapped my storyboard pitches and started over with traditional pitch bibles did I score my first development deal.

Love it or hate it, the pitch bible is the industry standard pitching format. In fact, the pitch bible can be such a powerful tool that it could actually sell your project without you ever having pitched in person. My

Gregory enters.
GREGORY
"Bradley, Your parents amuse me.
Your toys amuse me.
Your cookies… well, they are a little dry,
but, that's neither here nor there."

GREGORY
"The point is that YOU
have become a fly in my ointment."

BRAD
(grossed out)
"Ointment?"

GREGORY
"Know this Bradley! You cannot defy me!
No one can defy me, or disobey me!"

GREGORY (Cont)

"Bwa-Ha ha ha!"

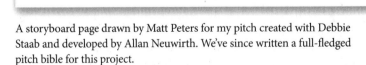

As Gregory explains, he whips out maps, charts, graphs…etc.

GREGORY
"Today, it's your house!"

A storyboard page drawn by Matt Peters for my pitch created with Debbie
Staab and developed by Allan Neuwirth. We've since written a full-fledged
pitch bible for this project.

first deal resulted from a pitch bible I e-mailed to a network executive. I hadn't even printed it out! Cartoon Network's *Codename: Kids Next Door* and *The Venture Bros.* were similarly pitched, via overnight mail.

Anatomy of a Pitch Bible

> "Your bible is a book. Be very aware of page turns, composition, balance, color, and readability. Oh, and be damn funny."

—**Mo Willems, creator of *Sheep in the Big City* (Cartoon Network)**

The nice thing about a two-sheet pitch proposal is that the length is predetermined: two sheets. The two-sheet's bigger cousin, the pitch bible, is harder to pin down. Just how long should it be? Development executive Peter Gal answers, "Long enough to sell the key characters, explain the main elements of the world and concept, and quickly convey some story premises." Doug TenNapel, creator of *Earthworm Jim* and *Catscratch*, reveals, "Every time I make too big of a bible, it just complicates the pitch, and that is the evil enemy of selling shows. So I've been working to strip my bibles down to usable, concise, powerful, truth statements about the show. It doesn't take much, and if your pitch requires a long bible, I'd be suspect of what you're pitching." So, a good rule of thumb might be to stick within the range of four to eight pages. Peter Gal suggests that length of the bible doesn't really matter, only content. "There are no hard-and-fast rules. Just show us your show!" he says.

oxymoron presents

the Monotony Variety Show.

 is our every-sheep. It's hard enough to make his way in the Big City without all the nuts chasing him!

16 10/6/99

SHEEP IN THE BIG CITY

*Another exciting adventure where **Sheep** balances the pressures of Big City life with being mercilessly hunted by a secret military organization.*

Swanky is Sheep's love interest. She's smarter than Sheep, but enjoys the attention he gives her. Like Sheep, she's barely anthropomorphic.

Little Bo Peep appears from time to time to recruit Sheep as her new sheep. Her cutesy-pie act drives Sheep Crazy.

more ➡

A sample character line-up page from Mo Willems's pitch bible for Cartoon Network's *Sheep in the Big City*. Note the uncluttered and playful page design. As Mo says, "Your bible is a book." *Sheep in the Big City*, its logo, and all related characters and elements are trademarks of and © 2008 The Cartoon Network.

I'm going to go out on a limb and say that there is, in fact, one hard-and-fast rule: A pitch book should be entertaining in and of itself. Remember, this is not a thesis paper or an article for the local news. You are attempting to bring a show to life before an executive's eyes, and it can't all be funny pictures. Like it or lump it, there need to be words! The words should be descriptive, conversational, and succinct. You've got to hook your reader in the first few sentences to get them to hunker down and explore the rest. The pitch book must capture the spirit of the show. Linda Simensky, vice president of children's programming at PBS, agrees: "If a pitch isn't interesting to read, the show probably won't be much better. Don't spend much of the pitch telling us how funny it will be, make it actually seem funny and that will go a long way in convincing us you have the right tone."

In a pitch book, less is more. Our challenge is to make sure less is more than enough. Creator Manny Galan experienced the "less is more" lesson first-hand. He explains, "Well in the beginning, I would create such incredibly detailed pitch bibles that [they] left no room for any executive or network to embellish the property in a way that made them feel they could perhaps make suggestions that could make it more suitable for their network. Also, no one wants to read a thirty-page document." *Assy McGee* co-creator Carl W. Adams agrees: "Keep it simple, because it is better to show too little and leave them wanting more rather than showing too much and turning them off with one small part of it."

The Cover

Despite the old parable, don't judge a book by its cover, that's exactly what may happen when it comes to pitch bibles. Take the time to make a graphically pleasing and professional cover that communicates the tone of the content and its designated audience. A preschool show should sport a cheery, colorful, friendly cover, while a pitch for Adult Swim should be decidedly darker and more, well, adult. One of the most successful TV cartoons of the past ten years was initially turned down by a network executive, but then scored a pick up when the network's vice president happened to notice the pitch book while visiting the executive's office. Casually thumbing through it before leaving for the weekend, the vice president said, "This is funny. Let's do this." A less graphically pleasing pitch book cover might have stayed on the desk, unnoticed and unloved.

THERE'S SOMETHING ABOUT GREGORY

The cover designed by my dad and me for the pitch I created with Debbie Staab, which was developed by Allan Neuwirth. A pitch bible cover should not only be attractive but should also set the tone for the show inside. We used a backwards "R" to match the show's Eastern European theme.

Series Log Line

"For me it all comes down to simplicity. Do you have a nice, clear, and most importantly, *interesting* premise that can be explained in one or two sentences?"

—**Tom Warburton, creator of *Codename: Kids Next Door* (Cartoon Network)**

Much like the two-sheet, the pitch bible should begin with a one-sentence series log line. I find it useful to think of familiar shows and practice writing log lines for them before you try to whittle your opus down to a sentence. A one-sentence log line for one of my favorite situation comedies, *The Odd Couple*, might read like this: "Can two divorced men share an apartment without driving each other crazy?" Note that the log line doesn't have to say everything. It's just a summary sentence, capturing the essence of the show in the most concise way possible. A series log line is not just a component of the pitch bible, it's also the first line spoken in a pitch meeting.

Series Synopsis

Next up is the series synopsis, and this is where you get to expand your log line into two paragraphs. The opening narration of *The Powerpuff Girls* would make a great short synopsis for the series: "Sugar, spice, and everything nice. These were the ingredients chosen to create the perfect little girls. But Professor Utonium accidentally added an extra ingredient to the concoction: Chemical X! Thus, the Powerpuff Girls were born. Using their ultra super powers, Blossom, Bubbles, and Buttercup have dedicated their lives to fighting crime and the forces of evil!"

However, there are some important synopsis elements missing from this overview. The reason *The Powerpuff Girls* is compelling is that our little trio struggles to balance its home and school life as preschoolers with the adult-sized task of protecting the city of Townsville. We also need a sample list of villains and their schemes, how the Powerpuff Girls are summoned into action each episode by a call from the bumbling mayor, and finally, the role of the omnipresent narrator, who helps tie all the elements of the show together.

Consider your own idea and all the pieces that come together to create the whole. It may not be necessary to include every supporting character and detail, but be sure to figure out which are necessary to your synopsis.

Format and the Rules of the World

Describing the format of your show could be the easiest part of the pitch bible. A format for one of my recent pitches read: "Animation comedy for kids, ages six to twelve. Two eleven-minute episodes in 2-D Flash stretch-and-squash-style animation, and featuring cutting-edge 3-D backgrounds created in Maya."

The first sentence addresses the genre of animation and the age of its intended audience. The second sentence explains the episode lengths and animation technique. The description "stretch-and-squash style-animation" has come to define a cartoony world, such as the one seen in

SpongeBob SquarePants, where the main character might do a double-take by splitting apart into two distinct halves and then reform into one body, good as new. Most live-action properties exist within the confines of the physics of the real world. Animation can be different. For instance, in *South Park,* Kenny may be killed at the end of every episode and revived for the next with no explanations needed. *The Simpsons* and *Family Guy* operate more like animated sitcoms and generally follow the physics and rules of the real world. For example, once Maude Flanders died, she was dead in all subsequent episodes.

Be sure to be clear and consistent about the world you're presenting and make sure everything else in the pitch bible supports these rules. All the elements of the pitch bible must work together in harmony. Linda Simensky says that creators often come up with very high-concept ideas that are interesting in the pitch for a few minutes, and then just seem like they take time away from the more important parts of the shows. She explains, "When someone pitches an idea where the world concept is highly stylized and everyone has names that are animals or plants or colors, I usually end up thinking that if I don't love the characters, I don't care how cleverly their world was constructed or how high their high concept was. Sometimes a world just isn't believable and a creator's defense is often, 'Well, this is my vision, [and] in this world, dogs fly. That's how I see it.' But there is often something missing or underdeveloped that makes you continue questioning the world."

Character Descriptions

"Try to avoid using too many adjectives in describing your characters. This can get muddy and doesn't really say who they are. One thing I did in a bible to avoid over-description was to pose twenty questions to the characters and have them answer in their own voices. It was better for me to have the characters express themselves than to have me talk about them."

—Craig McCracken, creator of *The Powerpuff Girls* and *Foster's Home for Imaginary Friends* (Cartoon Network)

What is the importance of strong characters in an animation pitch? Brown Johnson, president of animation at Nickelodeon, answers, "Good characters are the way the audience connects with TV (books, etc.). Characters need to be sympathetic, fully formed, and preferably fun. If there's a strong character at the heart of a show, the audience will stay engaged and tune in again." In a pitch book, you need to do more than describe a character—you need to bring that character to life. Saying a character is bossy, brainy, funny, irreverent, lazy, sloppy, dumb, curious, or any other adjective doesn't make it so. It is not proof or evidence of having created real characters. According to Brown Johnson, there is a handful of characters that show up in every pitch: "The brainy, assertive girl; the fat, happy one; the ADD, impulsive one; the shy one." Peter Gal agrees, "Often they are just a list of adjectives strung together or a description so familiar that it could fit a thousand different characters: 'She's the spunky girl who won't take no for an answer,' or 'He's the tech wiz [who] can fix anything.' We are looking for something much deeper."

Our job is to create and pitch real characters and describe them in a way that makes them leap off the page. If I were pitching a series based around Peter Falk's Lt. Columbo character, I'd want the development executive to smell Columbo's stale cigar and picture his mussed hair, rumpled raincoat, and five o'clock shadow. The artwork would show Columbo's seemingly confused brow, squinty, cock-eyed stare, and casual posture. The fun would be demonstrating the strange bedfellows of Columbo's shabby appearance and his brilliantly resourceful mind. Other elements of his character would be cemented by anecdotes about his wife, his difficulties training a disobedient dog, and his unusual attachment to a dilapidated, 1959 Peugeot 403 Grande Luxe Cabriolet (convertible). Legend has it that Falk selected the car himself after seeing it parked in the lot at Universal Studios. Each of these elements reveals or supports another aspect of the character's personality.

In a pitch bible, we should be able to describe a main character as rich as Falk's in two to three paragraphs of text accompanied by at least two or three illustrations. As a character writing exercise, Linda Simensky recommends writing a description of yourself the way you'd want to be described. "Most people have more than one or two character traits," she says. Peter Gal elaborates, "What are the strengths, weak-nesses, hopes, fears, dreams, vulnerabilities, pet peeves, odd habits, interests, passions, etc., of the character? What is that one key trait that will make this character funny and interesting to watch in almost any situation?"

the flirt

Real Name: Kuki Sanban
Specialty: Diversionary Tactics

- Cute, flirtatious, air headed, Japanese girl.
- Loud...so very, very loud.
- Only speaks Japanese yet everyone seems to understand her. Numbuh Four tends to repeat or answer everything she says in English anyway.
- Screams when excited, usually scaring the crap out of those nearby.
- Very forgetful and easily distracted by anything.
- Extremely afraid of flying.

Character page from Tom Warburton's pitch bible for *Codename: Kids Next Door*, boasting short and punchy descriptions of Numbuh Three. *Codename: Kids Next Door*, its logo, and all related characters and elements are trademarks of and © 2008 The Cartoon Network.

NUMBUH THREE

A t first you might think that Numbuh Three is just a little confused because she doesn't speak a word of English. But that's not it. Numbuh Three just happens to be in her own little world and is rarely paying attention to what is going on around her. In her case ignorance is supreme bliss. Always disgustingly cheery, Numbuh Three never fails to have fun at what she's doing, even if she doesn't know why she's doing it.

The reason she is involved with The KND is uncertain but she is willing to do anything, she takes orders well and doesn't ask any questions, which makes Numbuh One happy. Unfortunately, her incredibly short attention span has caused many a mission to go straight down the toilet.

Numbuh Three is terrified of flying, and she always causes a huge commotion when The KND have to take a plane to get somewhere. Which is often. So they usually have to trick her onto the plane in one way or another.

Numbuh Three falls madly in love with almost anyone but has a special place in her heart for a next door neighbor named Kenny. Probably only because he has a pet chimp.

Warburton gives us more prose about Numbuh Three in another page from his pitch bible. What? No mention of Rainbow Monkeys? *Codename: Kids Next Door*, its logo, and all related characters and elements are trademarks of and © 2008 The Cartoon Network.

The Perils of Back Story

Novelists, playwrights, and screenwriters often develop elaborate back stories to fully flesh out their character creations. In animation, some creators may wish to do the same. My advice is, while this may be a good writing exercise, don't let it creep directly into the pitch bible itself. In a pitch bible, characters must be described in the present. It would be a mistake to devote sentences and paragraphs to back story. Instead, concern yourself with making the characters come alive in active form.

I once made the mistake of filling an entire pitch book with the characters' back stories and psychology, which made my characters less real and "in the now." Development executives found it very difficult to wrap their heads around my creations because I told them what *made* the characters the way they are rather than telling them the way the characters are. When I pitched in person with a heavy emphasis on back story, the development executives' attention always drifted; they grew bored with the presentation. Nobody tunes in to *SpongeBob SquarePants* because of a desire to see that character's back-story, although that could make for an engaging episode. We watch *SpongeBob* because we want to spend time with that character and see him interact with other characters in his world.

As an employee of Nickelodeon in the late 1990s, I had the pleasure of seeing the first footage from the *SpongeBob* pilot. None of us in the room knew who SpongeBob was; there was no hype and there were no expectations. From the first scene, SpongeBob assaulted us with character, spending the first few minutes of the cartoon readying himself to meet his long-awaited destiny to be a fry cook at the Krusty Krab. SpongeBob lifted weights, exercised, and chanted, "I'm ready," for an endless amount of time. Here was a character throwing himself into a passionate frenzy to get a part-time, minimum-wage job at a fast food joint that the rest of us would be glad to get rid of. Overdeveloped passion or zest for the minor things in life was a key character trait of SpongeBob from the very beginning. This pilot film doesn't waste time showing the details of SpongeBob's origin. There's no reference to his parents, school, or troubled childhood. Instead, he is a character presented in full bloom, just being himself. If SpongeBob can make applying for a dead-end job funny and exciting, then he is the ultimate example of a successful character.

Show Art

> "Most pitch art is just not special. And that is the one thing it
> has to be. Good art, even great art, is often not good enough.
> The art needs to be different and exciting and convey the
> emotional and comedic life of the characters. I see a lot of
> very good art done by very talented artists who will have long,
> successful careers in this industry, but if they want their own
> [shows on networks], the art has to stand out and make a
> connection."
>
> —Peter Gal, development executive

How important is show art in an animated pitch? Tara Sorensen, vice
president of development, National Geographic Kids Entertainment,
answers, "Lackluster art really ends up sending the pitch in the wrong direction. Executives will evaluate the entire project based on the art (even
if you tell them the art is 'just inspirational'). If the network has an adverse
reaction to the art, they'll have an adverse reaction to your project, even if
the writing is strong enough to stand on its own." Development executive
Heather Kenyon adds, "In animation, a picture is worth 5,000 words. It
is so much easier to look at two characters interacting in a sketch and
understand their relationship—so much easier than [through] paragraphs
of writing. Ultimately, on the screen, it is that sketch that will show and
not strings of written adjectives."

There's a bonus documentary on the making of *SpongeBob SquarePants*
included in the season one DVD where creator Stephen Hillenburg
reveals that he hired some of his friends to create the show art for his
pitch bible. Imagine that: Stephen Hillenburg, a Cal Arts graduate, award-
winning filmmaker for his student film (*Wormholes*), and creative director
on Nickelodeon's *Rocko's Modern Life*, hired other artists to make the
show art for his pitch! Clearly, he understood the importance of show art.
Surely, he's a capable artist who could have handled the art himself, but
working with other artists may have opened Hillenburg's eyes to talents
that could help him best present his vision.

Development executives are surrounded by the best artistic talent in
the business and are used to seeing a professional standard of art. Heather
Kenyon agrees: "I will admit it—I am spoiled. I look at great art all day,

MR MEENIE
A K A FRENCH BREAD NOSE

Ensconced in his mountain institute in the Athlete foothills, Mr. Meenie is the most soft spoken of evil foes. He walks in little mincey steps and holds his arms up like a rabbit. His voice is half way between Peter Lorrie and Jackie Kennedy. Where Rasputini is loud and smelly, Mr. Meenie is sneaky clean. He carries germicidal sprays and is apt to spritz you during a conversation. Mr. Meenie is a super industrialist. He is not mainly out for money, though his sackfulls of it yearn for company. MM is a control freak, who wants to make people do what he wants them to when he wants them to. If you get in his way, you might just disappear (only to reappear weeks later in the polar bear cage at the zoo).

Debra Solomon's villain from her Cartoon Network pilot, *Private Eye Princess*. This pitch bible character page aptly demonstrates the show's style and the personality of the character, but I find the choice of font a little hard to read. *Private Eye Princess*, its logo, and all related characters and elements are trademarks of and © 2008 The Cartoon Network.

every day, and so when I get a pitch with art that isn't at that high, high level, it tends to make me think that the project isn't as professional." Take that into account when preparing show art for your pitch bible. Bring in help or collaborators where you need them. CartoonBrew.com's Jerry Beck has recruited help to make professional logo art for his pitch bibles. He adds, "I'm lucky enough to have several friends who design lettering and I find that a title treatment helps everyone visualize the project more professionally. I like to establish that my pitch is a 'real show,' that it is happening—whether your network picks it up or not."

For a two-sheet proposal, you may only need one or two pieces of show art. For a pitch bible, it would be a mistake not to feature art on every single page. Otherwise, you risk a pitch book filled with dull walls of type. Show art should help communicate and support the characters and world you have created. This is one area where we can't count on development executives to use their imaginations. Instead, show art should visually depict the characters, their world, and selected plot descriptions in a way that allows all the elements to work together. The show art must also be able to stand on its own even outside of the pitch book. *Codename: Kids Next Door* creator Tom Warburton agrees: "I always tell people to think about what their promo drawing for the show would be. Could they see it in a magazine or on a kiosk in a mall?" Similarly, Doug TenNapel likes to think of his lead characters as stickers. "I look at my main character and think back to being in sixth grade and say, 'Man, I wish I had a sticker of this guy to put on my math book!' Good characters look emblematic and have to represent something bigger than the initial appeal of a first take."

Continuing with my example of Peter Falk's Lt. Columbo character, it's easy to imagine how fun (and enlightening) it would be to see show art of some of his signature poses. I'm instantly imagining his famous "One more thing" pose, with arm outstretched in the direction of the murder suspect. There's also his signature hand-on-straining-brow pose. Additionally, we'd be sure to include full views of Columbo, head to foot, to reveal the detective in all his scruffy glory. And we'd provide images of the detective that show him as a fish out of water, contrasting his shabby exterior with his posh surroundings. Last, we'd include at least one image of Columbo in his beat-up car, which almost seems like an extension of the character himself. These images are descriptive and full of character and conflict, and they feature the character interacting with

Sam is the monkey-wrench in his own plans. A rabbit with an overactive imagination filled with ideas of soaring rocketships, for instance. But, his mind gets too eager to let him just sit back and dream about rockets. With all those rockets in his head, the only thing he can do is slap together a spaceship and assemble a "crew" from his group of friends.

Sam's tunnel-vision in carrying out his plans keeps hi from really planning the little details... like using the correct rocket-fuel, safety precautions, or any technical knowledge... instead he is ready to roll up his sleeves and get to work with a box of old vacuum cleaner parts, a few crude hand-drawn maps to the moon and a box of astronaut ice-cream.

Sam's can-do, unquestioning attitude rubs off onto his friends till they're working together to turn their bicycles into motorbikes, then someone's backyard into a motorbike stunt course, then making trophies out of their demolished motorbikes.

Who else would have thought of the plan to use a refrigerated truck as their summertime clubhouse and then forgotten that the truck would be filled with frozen scrod bound for Iowa City? Or the plan to make giant cartoon costumes as a disguise to get into the amusement park for free... but accidentally using characters for a competing park... which caused a hilarious brawl on Main Street, USA. Or the plan to get the roof of his house re-covered in rubber so that it would become a giant trampoline with no regard for the study of trajectories.

If his school class were presenting a play, he would be the first one to try to direct it, and then run into trouble when the principal finds out about all the explosions, fake blood, latex prosthetic makeup, and gross literary inaccuracies. At least that's what happened last time. It was the best "Midsummer Night's Dream" ever.

He tried to alter his genes by microwaving popcorn while standing next to a radio tower as they were broadcasting "Monster Mash," in order to mutate into something good for Halloween. He tried to get his pals to hitchhike to where fireworks are legal. He tried to get them all to get jobs as lumberjacks for the breakfast specials. He spent several weeks slowly switching all the parts of his dad's car to his bicycle.

Although Sam's friends are all smart underachievers at school Sam is the one in the group that is not, in all honesty "smart." This helps the others in his group of friends that can get too caught-up in "thinking."

Sam lives with his Mom and Dad. He's an only child, which is rather rare for rabbits. He is the most innocent and unjaded of his group of friends. The reason he comes up with such crazy plans is that it never crosses his mind that they might not be possible, and his contagious enthusiasm for hare-brained schemes gets his friends involved.

A character page from Fran and Will Krause's pitch for *The Upstate Four*. The pose is a lot of fun, but most experts agree to stay away from walls of text. Happily, a pitch bible doesn't have to be perfect, and the Krauses scored a pilot based on their considerable talents. *The Upstate Four*, its logo, and all related characters and elements are trademarks of and © 2008 The Cartoon Network.

his world. This is the very role of show art in your pitch bible. However, there's no need to do an endless amount of art. Butch Hartman, *The Fairly OddParents* creator, advises making only one or two drawings of each character and the same for the world. Linda Simensky recommends that your drawings should not simply be posed for a presentation or as part of a character lineup, because they can look pretty static. "The optimum pitch, from my point of view, has rough art as well as finished art, and shows characters in a variety of situations or actions. If the show is meant to be humorous, the designs should convey that," she says.

In an animated project, the world itself is often like a character and should be treated as such in the show art. A great example of this is Bikini Bottom, the undersea world of *SpongeBob SquarePants,* which is filled with drifting bubbles, nutty architecture (like SpongeBob's pineapple house), and boat-like cars that drive along the ocean floor. Virtually anything that could be found above ground has a counterpart in Bikini Bottom. There is even an appeal to the way each bit of coral is designed. This very inviting world with unlimited potential is a key component of why *SpongeBob SquarePants* scored a pick up, and also why it's been so incredibly successful.

I feel the need to stress that, because this is an animation pitch, the show art should be rendered in the style of your show's animation. A 2-D flash animated show pitch should not feature 3-D rendered show art. The development executive will look at each of your show art images as if it was ripped right out of the show itself. These images represent what the show might look like on the air. Be sure you present the show as it best fits the material along with the medium or animation technique you intend to use. Whatever your style of animation, Carl H. Greenblatt advises that the important thing is to make development executives *feel* something. "If they laugh, then you've got them on your side."

The Plot Thickens: Episode Synopses in a Pitch Bible

"Generic stories can be told in any series, and we have all seen them before, so they're not going to get us excited. We are looking for premises that are very unique to these characters and, in a sense, could only be told in this way on this show."

—Peter Gal, development executive

A common complaint I've heard from nearly all development executives is that too often a promising pitch bible falls apart at the key area of sample episode ideas. Most often the problem is that the bible excels at describing interesting characters and promising setups and worlds, but then utilizes little to none of it in the sample plots provided. It's as if the creator ran out of steam or lacked the necessary writing chops to demonstrate a typical episode in action. I've also heard this problem described as telling rather than showing that the character is funny.

There's also an automatic skepticism on the development executive's part when they are told that a character will be funny. Saying something doesn't make it so. Some friends of mine perusing online dating sites have complained about a similar phenomenon in terms of personal ad profiles. So many people describe themselves as smart and funny, but so few live up to that reputation in their filled-in answers. The same is true in a pitch book. All of us, in turn, say our characters are funny, smart, dumb, messy, impatient, bossy, rude, silly, or grumpy. The plots are where a creator proves that her characters and concept are ripe for exploring and not only shows how all the elements stitch together but also proves that the plots themselves are born out of character and character interactions. It's easy to understand why the sample episode ideas do some of the heavy lifting in a pitch bible.

I've had some fun discussions with executives who place all emphasis on character alone. They like to hold Bugs Bunny as a shining example of a great character because he is resourceful, confident, funny, and infallible. If I didn't know Bugs Bunny, I'd say, based on that description alone, that he is terribly boring. Who wants to spend time with a character that always wins? I find it difficult to imagine how a character that always wins is funny in the first place. Can you imagine spending a day inside with Bugs Bunny? A day where no hunters stick their gun barrel down his rabbit hole? A day when no thick-necked construction worker tries to build on the hare's land? I can imagine it, and it sounds like a yawn-fest.

Based on pure character and description alone, there is nothing exceptional about Bugs Bunny. The magic of Bugs only comes to life as the character is activated by the machinations of plot. The plot, when it does come, is simple and exists only to set the characters into conflict so that the sparks and fur may fly. One plot depicts a familiar situation: a hunter hunting a rabbit. The characters provide the twist: the prey is smarter than the hunter. Remember, there's nothing funny about a hunter sticking a gun into the ground to kill a rabbit; what's funny is how Bugs reacts to the danger he's in, which allows his character to rise to the occasion.

The pattern was set in what is widely regarded as the first full-fledged *Bugs Bunny* cartoon, *A Wild Hare* (1940), directed by the legendary Tex Avery: Elmer tracks his prey to a rabbit hole, places a juicy carrot just out of the hole's reach, and waits nearby with a ready shotgun. Bugs instantly turns the tables on the hunter by snatching the carrot before Elmer can react, engaging his gun barrel in a tug of war, and finally ruining the weapon by magically tying it in a bow. All this happens before Bugs has even fully emerged from his hole! Throughout the rest of the picture, Bugs continues to outsmart and humiliate the dimwitted Elmer in a variety of ways, including mockery, guessing games, insult kisses, impersonating a stinky skunk, and even feigning cooperation by pretending to give Elmer a clean shot at him.

Such a classic, theatrical, seven-minute format can be broken down into three parts: Bugs is at peace, Bugs is provoked, Bugs gives 'em hell. Today's TV cartoon is usually a half-hour show, divided up into two separate eleven-minute stories. Therefore a more relevant model than Bugs Bunny might be *SpongeBob SquarePants*. Let's try breaking down the *SpongeBob SquarePants* episode called "The Paper" to see how a modern character-driven cartoon takes shape. "The Paper" breaks down as follows:

- Squidward discards an ordinary piece of paper.

- SpongeBob relentlessly begs him for custody of the bit of paper, explaining all the fun one could have with such a thing.

- Squidward, who sees the paper as trash, easily gives in and lets SpongeBob have it, and in an attempt to quickly get rid of his annoying neighbor, promises the paper to SpongeBob "forever." Squidward also (sarcastically) asks SpongeBob to promise not to give the paper back to him, no matter how much he begs and pleads.

- SpongeBob delights himself to no end and finds endless ways to enjoy the paper, including using it as jungle pants, a parachute, a bull-fighter's cape, a mustache, an eye patch, etc.

- Squidward is first annoyed, then jealous, then full of regret that he gave away such a wonderful piece of paper.

- Squidward asks for the paper back, but SpongeBob can't comply because to do so would be to break his promise.

- Squidward finally trades all his earthly possessions, including the very shirt on his back, to get the paper back. Finally tempted beyond the breaking point, SpongeBob agrees to the trade.

- Much too late, Squidward finally realizes his folly—he's traded away everything he owns for a useless scrap of paper, which, it turns out, the squid is not equipped to do anything with.

To better appreciate the storyline above, let's quickly recap SpongeBob's personality. The little yellow square dude is an innocent, loud, creative, man-child who sees the world through a pair of over-eager

He's little, he's yellow, he's different . . . he's SpongeBob SquarePants! Copyright 2008, Viacom International, Inc. All rights reserved.

eyes. His long-suffering neighbor is his polar opposite. Squidward is refined, adult, cranky, stiff, and unimaginative.

SpongeBob SquarePants creator Stephen Hillenburg explains that the humor should always come from character, and the characters can be built upon with silly concepts: "SpongeBob and Patrick both have candy bars. Patrick is so stupid that he forgets that he has just eaten his and believes the one SpongeBob holds was his. SpongeBob is now a thief."

It's important to note that a character-based plot created for use on *SpongeBob* would not be something that could also be used for *Codename: Kids Next Door*, for instance. *Codename: Kids Next Door*'s stories are driven by its own characters' particular idiosyncrasies. None of this means that plot ideas have to be wholly original. All that is required is that plots come from character and reveal more information about the characters as it throws them into conflict. A simple question you might ask yourself is: Does my plot spring from character?

You Say You Want a Resolution

> "My pet peeve is episode ideas that end with: "Find out what happens when . . ." or a string of questions. "Will Larry save the day?" I don't know. Will he? You have told me that Larry is this great ingenious guy who is clever and fantastic. Okay, so how does he save the day? Now is your time to prove it. Prove that your characters are interesting and resourceful."
>
> —Heather Kenyon, development executive

Former Cartoon Network development executive Alex Manugian recently criticized a pitch bible of mine because it contained several examples of plot synopses that did not come to resolution. He pointed out that the resolutions were key because they would give much-needed insight into the characters and how they solve their particular problems. In fact, it was especially true because my pitch featured a main character who was supposed to scrape by on his resourcefulness in the face of ridiculously huge obstacles. Plot ideas should not be presented like the "to be continued" endings from *The Rocky and Bullwinkle Show*. Heather Kenyon explains, "I am really looking for a beginning, middle, and end that show the characters and their personalities driving the stories—which are unique to your particular world." As for the number of plot ideas to include in a pitch bible, I have found that a minimum of six and a maximum of ten plots is a good rule of thumb. I like to explain each plot in three short paragraphs.

Heather Kenyon stresses that episode ideas are really your chance to drive an interesting concept and well-defined characters home. She concludes, "Episode ideas frequently make or break a pitch. I have read your series overview, I have met all of your characters, now how does all this come together and form a unique and interesting show?"

Contact Info/Bios

The last part of a pitch book should be a page listing your complete contact information. If there are multiple creators, make sure to include only one as the main contact, for simplicity's sake. The contact info should include your complete name, address, home phone, cell phone, fax, e-mail, and any pertinent Web site address. Also use this page to list a short biography for each principal creator on the project (keep them to one paragraph each). This bio should primarily be a work history mixed with any notable achievements such as film festival awards. It won't hurt to make these bios as fun, punchy, and readable as possible. My feeling is that any bit of writing in a pitch bible should convey the creator's unique and interesting point of view, making for an informative and entertaining read.

The Preschool Pitch Bible

The pitch bible for a preschool series would follow all the guidelines listed above, only adding one key difference to the mix: a description of the show's intended curriculum. Curriculum is the educational component of a preschool series, which might promote the viewers' development in the areas of math, reading, grammar, spelling, cognitive reasoning, physical fitness, nutrition, social skills, cultural diversity, environmental awareness, etc.

For my pitch bible for *Fiona Finds Out*, my first project to score a development deal, the curriculum section read: "*Fiona Finds Out* features a cognitive reasoning curriculum [that encourages] preschoolers' (ages two to six) development of organized thought, logic, reasoning and problem solving. By utilizing an interactive format in which the home viewer is a vital participant in the show, *Fiona Finds Out* empowers preschoolers to discover their own untapped potential to imagine, explore, understand, and connect with the world in a fun, new, and exciting way!"

Creators would be advised to research the validity of their chosen curricula and might want to mention educational experts or studies that back them up. However, a pitch bible curriculum need not be outlined in more detail than my example above. Once a development deal is struck, a child development research analyst will be engaged to expand upon the series' curriculum, although some creators may wish to consult with such a specialist before the pitching process.

Pitch Bible Extras

A pitch bible extra is anything additional (besides a pitch bible) that you might present in a pitch meeting. It could be your creation in comic book form, storyboard, or script. In fact, I think these might be among the best pitch extras you could create. Short of making an actual pilot, nothing brings all the elements of your pitch bible together like a script or storyboard of a sample episode. You've got to be very careful, however. It's important that these extra materials show off your project in the best possible light. Much like Stephen Hillenburg enlisting help on his show art, you may want to lean on a professional writer and storyboard artist to make your script or storyboard shine. The bottom line is that these materials should not be less than what the development executive might picture in his imagination. In fact, a poor (or even average) script or storyboard could lower your chances of scoring a development deal.

I find writing a script and preparing a storyboard to be very useful exercises that help me understand my creation better than making just a pitch book does. The goal (and the challenge) here is to script a typical episode; for example, episode eleven out of an entire season of shows. Never, under any circumstances, begin by writing the origin story: how all the characters met or become involved in their current situation. Origin stories might be fun to explore in a second season of a series, but they make very poor pitch documents because they don't offer a glimpse of a typical episode. Instead, start all the characters engaged in a plot that would work at any point in the series. Imagine a new TV viewer tuning in to an episode of Cartoon Network's *The Powerpuff Girls* midway through the second season. This viewer will probably be able to understand what is going on even though, for this person, all the show's elements are in play for the first time. This is what your sample script or storyboard needs to conjure.

Be sure that whatever pitch extra you create works in harmony with the essence of your idea. Creator Manny Galan had great success with a pitch booklet about a superhero that featured his character and support-ing cast in a story in the form of a full-color, ten-page comic book. Galan adds, "It was a fun and easy read that conveyed everything you [needed] to know about the character and his world. It proved very effective and it got us an option."

The next most common pitch book extra is a bit of finished animation that represents a glimpse of what the finished show might look like. While this can be a great sales tool, it can also be a huge disaster. All the experts agree that one should not show finished animation unless it's absolutely perfect and represents what a finished version of the show might look and sound like in all its splendor. If it is anything short of that, do not show it! Speaking of short, when it comes to showing animation as a

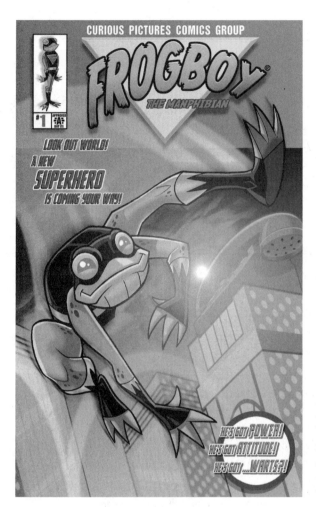

Manny Galan's pitch book extra, a comic book that brought his project to life in active form and helped score him a development deal. Image courtesy of the artist.

pitch element, the shorter the better. Do not exceed more than one or two minutes. As for content, choose a self-contained bit of business that reveals the main character's personality and conflict.

Other pitch bible extras might include original songs, recordings of a character's voice, and maybe a lock of your hair. Okay, that last one is a joke. Any extras you include should further the understanding of your pitch. Again, if your extras are not better than what a development executive might imagine in his or her own head, then don't show them! Additionally, pitch extras should never be the emphasis or main point of a pitch. Peter Gal explains, "I would much rather have the creator take the time they would have spent on that presentation and spend it thinking about their characters and finding the deeper, funnier layers to those characters."

Pitch Bible No-Nos

The simple definition of a pitch bible no-no would be any amount of time spent on areas that were not listed in this chapter. The above components of a pitch bible are the essentials—the necessary avenues that any animation pitches must navigate successfully to score a development deal. While there's no such thing as an exact science when it comes to pitching, most creators and development executives agree that a pitch bible should stay away from listing reasons why the network must buy the show or displaying marketing facts and figures. Heather Kenyon adds, "Let's figure out who the character is before we start putting him or her on a T-shirt."

Kenyon continues, "Please: no faux merchandise, no pets along for the pitch, no bubble machines, no mimes, no . . . you get the idea. Just print out what you have on your computer and bring it in. I have never liked something due to hoopla. I have, however, optioned something in the room based on a sketch in a very well-used and loved sketchbook."

Some creators believe it will help their pitch about green fluffy monsters if they cover their pitch book with green fur. Linda Simenksy reveals, "I personally have no particular interest in how well the show is packaged if I don't fall in love with the basic idea. I have never picked up a show because it was packaged well for the pitch. I have wondered in some cases if the person behind the pitch might be better suited for a marketing job at times. . . . We have an ongoing joke about people who have their projects professionally bound at the printer's because the first thing we usually do is tear the binding off to have copies made."

Chapter 4

Legal

"More often than not, the negotiation of a deal comes down
to a single word: leverage. How badly does the party you're
negotiating with want or need what you have to offer versus
how willing are you to walk away from the negotiation if that
party is not willing to meet your terms?"

—**Robert D. Marcus, Esq.**

Before we can discuss where and when a creator's legal needs begin,
there's one important myth-conception to mash: a notion that I call "the
great rip-off myth." Among the most common rookie questions concerning pitching is, "How do I protect my creation?" My default short answer
is, "You don't." You don't protect a creation; you develop, nurture, and
freely pitch a creation. Copyright questions and the fear of getting ripped
off prevent many would-be creators from getting off the ground. It's easy
to imagine our precious little babies getting stolen right from under us
by some smiling, back-stabbing executive. The truth is, in animation,
this seldom (if ever) happens. There's a far more likely scenario that is far
less dramatic: the idea that you brought in about an opera-singing robot

*Disclaimer: Although the material included in this chapter provides general guidance in the
area of legal contracts, it is not to be construed as the rendering of legal advice and does not
create any attorney-client relationship between myself or any of the people contributing their
opinions and advice.*

sheriff with an Oedipal complex in a futuristic Wild West has been passed across the development executive's desk twice that week already! Well, not the exact idea, but something quite similar.

Still unconvinced? A friend of mine developed a neat idea about a family of spies and spent months creating a lush series bible with juicy show art, a full script, and all the other trimmings. On the very first attempt at pitching this to Nickelodeon, the development executive told my friend, "This is great. Unfortunately, we're already doing something very similar called *The X's*." It's now more than five years later and *The X's* still has yet to set the world on fire (it was canceled after a year), but that's beside the point. The show was made and broadcast. Was my friend ripped off in reverse by a series that was already in production because he conceived something in the same vein? This is what happens, folks. We all breathe the same air. We are products of the same world. You could say that good ideas are flowing in the cosmos, making it all the more important to seize the moment when inspiration strikes. To me, sitting on an idea, worried that vultures are waiting to pounce upon it, is a waste of creativity.

The examples are many. Not too long ago, I prepared a pitch proposal for a preschool series. I was just about ready to set up a pitch meeting with a friendly network, when I got wind that that same network was picking up a new preschool project by a friend of mine. When a mutual friend of ours described that project to me, I was alarmed that it had shades of my proposal in it. In my experience, I knew that I hadn't been ripped off, nor had I ripped off my friend. Instead, I got the sinking feeling that someone had gotten there ahead of me and that now the door would be closed. At a panel on pitching at the Platform Festival, former Nickelodeon development executive Peter Gal remarked, "If a network tells you they are passing on your idea because they already have something similar, it's probably just a nice way to let you down gently. Actually, networks will pick up several similar projects for development because nobody knows which project is going to take off." Peter Gal makes a good point, but a network's development resources and budget can only be spread so far.

Happily, my project in the above story eventually sold elsewhere, finding a happy network home, albeit only a temporary one. A few short months after my deal was signed, I'd written one fully approved script and gotten approval on four additional premises. In development meetings, the network executive and I gradually abandoned the first proposed

Art from my pitch, *Fiona Finds Out*. This project shared key traits with one project already in development at one network and had a script similar to an episode of another series. Such coincidences are frequent in the world of development and should not be misconstrued as rip-offs.

pilot script that had been part of the original pitch elements. Imagine my shock, a few months later, to be sitting in a dentist's waiting room where I saw a very similar script appear on a network preschool show. Obviously, the show's script would have been at least a year old if it had just hit television. That would make it a little older than my first typed draft. As the cliché goes, there's nothing new under the sun.

Seemingly quirky, offbeat ideas are not immune to this universal law either. Frederator development executive Eric Homan was astonished to see two similar ideas pitched to him from two different creators in the same week. Both pitches featured central characters with fish bowls in place of where their heads should be. Again, there's no victim, just the collective consciousness at work.

Networks seek to protect themselves by requiring creators to fill out submission release forms prior to pitching. In this form, the creator provides information such as the title and description of the pitch. By signing the submission release form, which does not require the services of a lawyer, the creator testifies that he is the sole originator of the material and has full right to submit the material to the network under the terms the form defines. Another important clause indemnifies the network against any claims the creator may make against the network concerning the pitch materials submitted. While this may sound like cause for alarm, it's an obvious and necessary basic protection for a network. Besides, a creator already has her own form of basic protection as the copyright holder of her own work. In the rare event that you have a liability against the network, you can still pursue your claim with legal action.

As a closing thought on the great rip-off myth, here is a revelation I had while attending a Women in Animation panel on animation artists that have transitioned into becoming published authors. As typically happens at these events, many audience members asked questions about the dangers of companies or individuals stealing their ideas. They wondered how to protect themselves. The panelists, Tom Warburton, Megan Montague Cash, and Allan Neuwirth, calmly allayed their fears. The consensus was that it's extremely unlikely that anyone's ideas will be stolen. And on the off chance that it does happen, you can always sue. Simple enough.

The revelation I had was that it's not really paranoia or lack of experience in the industry that makes people worry about being ripped off. Focusing on this concern says something else entirely: you are way too precious with your idea, and chances are it's your only idea. It's no good to obsess on any one particular idea and overprotect it. Real creativity doesn't work that way. Writers and creators learn their craft and develop their voice by constantly creating new things. Any successful creator will tell you about his sketchbooks or drawers filled with ideas for scripts, books, shows, comics, etc. Worrying about the unlikely event of being ripped off is just another form of self-sabotage that keeps you from really taking a chance on your dream.

When Does a Creator Need a Lawyer?

Accident victims have it easy: not only are their needs for legal representation relatively clear, but they also have the option of picking an attorney from the gaggle of lawyers tailing their ambulance. For creators who are developing and pitching projects, legal representation is a product of need. As an individual creator, you don't need a lawyer to create, develop, and pitch a project. However, for projects created or developed by two or more persons, it is highly recommended that you create a binding agreement between parties prior to pitching.

Entertainment lawyer Robert Marcus explains, "This is sort of the last thing that two people working together usually think about because they are too busy doing what they're skilled at: creating stories, drawing characters, and otherwise being creative as they shape the vision of what they hope will be the next big thing. I recommend that up front, as early as possible, co-creators establish their relationships and roles on the project—before they pitch. You don't want to get a phone call and have the network say, "We want it," and then the two creators look at each other and say, 'Well this was really my idea,' or, 'This part was my idea.' Is it a fifty-fifty or some other split on the creation? They should have a collaboration agreement setting forth their respective rights and obligations in writing."

But do partnering creators need to hire an entertainment lawyer to draft up a collaboration agreement? A contract is simply an agreement between two parties. Courts will enforce an agreement if it's clear what the parties agreed upon. While it is legal to write your own contract, it's not always in your best interest, outside of saving legal fees. The most important concern when drafting a contract is that it be clear, be precise, and cover all the bases. An agreement allows all parties to understand their respective rights and obligations to one another. As much as there seem to be no universal truths when it comes to animation pitching and development, one thing is fairly certain: creators should seek out legal help when they find themselves with a development deal offer.

Leverage is a two-sided coin. What's important to keep in mind is that the network is not only buying an idea or concept, it is also (more importantly) buying the creator's passion, vision, point of view, and—if the project goes forward—execution. A creator with a track record in the industry is perceived as less of a risk. The lower the risk, the greater the network's desire to cut a deal, and the greater the amount of leverage possessed by the creator for negotiating purposes. Rob Marcus advises clients who are just starting out to not necessarily walk away from a deal or feel too dejected if the financial terms will mean that they'll have to put off buying their mansion for a few years. "Although they'll need to review and evaluate all of the terms of the agreement you're presented with, you've got to get your foot in the door and into the creative stream, which will hopefully increase your leverage for the next deal," he says.

I attended a pitching and development panel at the first Platform International Animation Festival, where I heard then–Nickelodeon development executive Peter Gal remark, "If it's your first deal, there's not much point to negotiating. It is what it is." I heard this point and immediately thought of my network deal, on which the ink was still fresh at the time. My lawyer and I had negotiated and significantly improved the deal, which had resulted in much higher rates and an all-around better contract. After the panel, I approached Mr. Gal and explained how, despite being an untested creator, I was able to greatly improve my first development deal through negotiation. Mr.Gal responded, "Well, yes. That's because you're established." Happily, even though this was my first network development deal, my twelve-year (and counting) career as a storyboard artist, animator, designer, illustrator, author, and director counted for something. Not only did it help create some leverage in the negotiation process, but one could argue my experience helped serve as the catalyst for the deal itself.

If You Rep Yourself, You Might Wreck Yourself

Cute heading aside (and I am proud of it), should creators ever attempt to handle the legal work and negotiate a deal themselves? I would answer, definitely not—although readers of my first book may recall that I opted to negotiate my ill-fated first development deal. In that case, the deal was so lame and the money so small that an attorney would have set me back thousands of dollars on a project that had little chance of going anywhere.

Years later, when I was offered a proper development deal from a television network, I enlisted the legal services of Rob Marcus to represent

Bill Plympton, the author, and John Andrews enjoy drinks during a break at the Platform International Animation Festival. Festivals offer lots of opportunities for networking, which can be very handy to creators and network executives alike. Photo credit by Biljana Labovic.

me and negotiate all the points of the deal. Working with him was educational. He had limitless patience while fielding my many questions, and always took the time to make sure I understood every important detail in the contracts. In the end, my attorney was able to increase all the creator fees, ensure my continued attachment to the project, and even build in a clause that guaranteed payment for certain services if the network decided to abandon my project or to move forward without me and have someone other than me render those services. A short time later, this clause required the network to pay me for full design services even though by that time they'd pulled the plug on the project. As an added benefit, that particular sum ended up covering the legal costs on the whole development deal. If I had represented myself, I would have never even known that such a point of negotiation existed.

Another important reason to *not* represent yourself in the negotiation process is the importance of preserving good relationships with the development executives, their networks, and their attorneys. Rob Marcus advises, "At the end of the day, it's important to separate yourself because of the old 'good cop, bad cop,' cliché. Unlike closing on a house where the purchaser and the seller go their separate ways and never see each other again, when the option [or] development agreement is done, you actually have to work with the company. My negotiation style is to vigorously and diligently represent my clients but also be reasonable. I have no problem going back to the negotiation again and again on a particular point if something is unreasonable. I don't know if the other side appreciates that I won't simply take 'no' for answer, but I have found that it's better for me to be the lawyer [or] bad cop by doing the asking."

Marcus continues, "At the same time I don't necessarily want to leave the other side with a bad taste from the negotiation because, at the end of the day, they're going to have to work with my client. Hence, when asking and then, if necessary, asking again for points that might have been initially shot down, it's extremely important to be able to provide a sound explanation as to why I feel so strongly about the position I'm advocating." TV packaging agent and entertainment lawyer Jim Arnoff agrees that negotiating is usually a mess when people try to do it alone. "Negotiations can be emotional and you could sour a creative relationship by doing your own negotiations," he says.

Right about now you may be asking, "How important is it to have an entertainment lawyer who has experience negotiating animation deals?" Robert Marcus answers, "You want to have somebody versed with the parameters of what's customary in this particular industry. A music lawyer, although very versed in contracts, would be much more familiar with the parameters for royalties and advances in the music industry but would not likely be equally versed in what the parameters are for the animation industry."

Jim Arnoff similarly cautions that an entertainment lawyer dealing only with the live action film industry wouldn't know how to articulate terms specific to animation deals. He explains, "You need to know the animation lingo, the different delivery dates, and the way fees are paid at certain stages of production. Are there ancillary or merchandising rights? What is your participation? If my client is doing artwork, how many revisions? What are the deliverables? How many characters? What format?" According to Arnoff, the basics are the same for animation and live action contracts, but how you define them will be different. The point is that a live action lawyer wouldn't know how to articulate the animation-specific terms.

Finding a Lawyer

Since enlisting a lawyer is a result of need, it's doubtful that you'll know one before you need one. However, anyone working in the animation industry on another creator's show knows someone who can recommend a good entertainment lawyer with experience in animation.

You might also encounter an attorney by attending industry panels and events. As ASIFA-East president, I hosted an event with then–Cartoon Network development executive Heather Kenyon, where an unfamiliar voice in the audience kept asking especially savvy legal questions.

After the event, I learned that the voice belonged to entertainment attorney Robert Marcus, who had accompanied his client, my friend Xeth Feinberg, to the event. I subsequently learned that Marcus had also represented other New York–based creators, such as Fran and Will Krause and John R. Dilworth. He had been instrumental in negotiating on behalf of J. J. Sedelmaier's animation studio during the first season of *Beavis & Butt-Head* in addition to representing my friend Melanie Grisanti in her first deal working in animation as a producer on Jim Jinkins's series *Doug*. Needless to say, Marcus knew animation deals. I kept him in the back of my mind, and two months later he was my attorney, representing me on my option-and-services deal with a cable television network.

It's hammer time! A still from Xeth Feinberg's zany (or should I say, "xany") indie Web toon series, *Papu*, which is written, produced, and distributed by the artist. Image courtesy of the artist.

However you find a lawyer, you should be sure that she will represent you the way you want to be represented. Arnoff adds, "It's still important for a client to be involved in the whole process. You want to educate yourself, collaborate with your lawyer. It's teamwork, and since you pick your team, it's a reflection of you. Be sure to go with someone you trust and who will return your phone calls. You have to assume your lawyer will be a cheerleader, [an] ally, and a key to your success."

The Option

Most development deals start with an option. Whether it's live action or animation, what you're starting with is a creator's property. It's not common for the purchaser, producer, production company, or network to say, "We love it. We're going to make it." Instead, they're going to option it, which, as Rob Marcus says, is basically a way for the network to say, "'We like your idea and want to have the opportunity to develop it further, [but] we don't yet want to commit the amount of money we'd have to commit if we decide to go forward with it.' Hence, they'll pay you a negotiated amount of money *now* to option your property for a specified negotiated period of time, usually with an option to extend the period for an additional negotiated payment. If at any time prior to the expiration of the option period they decide to go forward with the project, they will have the right to exercise the option by paying you a negotiated purchase price."

The next logical question is, How long a period of time might a typical option cover? Marcus describes this as a balancing act: "As the lawyer representing the creator, I don't want the option period to be for too long, particularly if there is not a lot of money changing hands for the option period. I typically want to feel that the party optioning my client's property is motivated to actually develop it and not have it gathering dust on a shelf. . . . On the other hand, the reality is that projects rarely move from development to a greenlight as quickly as one would like. Hence, you don't typically want to insist on an unrealistically short option period. Remember, the end goal is not to simply collect option payments, but to get your project produced, which will then trigger payment of the purchase price and, ideally, other obligations to you (including credit, fees for additional services, and some form of back-end participation)." (Back-end participation means that, in addition to the upfront fees paid to a creator, you receive a cut of the royalties or fees culled from secondary distribution channels and ancillary products.)

Marcus explains that although there is no standard, you should expect to option your property for an initial period of one year with an option to extend the period for another year. Ideally, you'll want to make sure your services are retained to help develop the property, which will, as Marcus says, "put additional fees in your pocket and keep you involved creatively." Services can include character designs, a bible, story premises, and storyboards.

"Ideally, although [this is] not typically the case, during the option period they'll also commit to produce a short based on those development items. If the company will not commit to produce a short they would likely, in the alternative, require the right to produce one during the option period," Marcus concludes. Either way, your contract should give you the right to render services and [to] be paid a fee for these services on the short. This is not automatically given, as this point often needs to be negotiated by your lawyer. As for any additional creative services that you'll be providing, Rob Marcus points out that "they will most likely be rendered as a work-for-hire, which essentially means that under copyright law, the company that you are doing the work for will be the legal copyright owner of the results and proceeds of your services. However, I strongly recommend trying to negotiate a provision in the option agreement that allows you to acquire the rights to the materials you prepared as works for hire. Although this will most likely require some payment, having the rights to these development materials could prove very helpful to have should you subsequently try to set the project up elsewhere down the line."

Marcus concludes, "At the end of the day, we can't lose sight of the big picture. The big picture is not [to] get a couple of extra thousands of dollars, but to get them to love the project, love you, and exercise the option and keep you attached to the project [for] as long a period as possible." Marcus encourages his animation clients who are new to the business to think of the opportunity offered to them as a continuation of their film school experience. "Look at it this way: you are now having some third party pay you to develop a property of yours," he says.

Legal Fees

From a creator's vantage point, signing a development deal—and even going all the way to making a pilot—is no way to earn a living. As far as the networks, Web destinations, or production companies are concerned, development is speculative and exploratory, and this is reflected in the low monetary compensation offered to the creator. Obviously, the less prior experience a creator has, the lower the development and option fees will be.

Most creators shouldn't expect to be earning a lot of money during development deal options and work-for-hire services periods. Since good entertainment lawyers don't come cheap, a creator's meager earnings will be split further. Costs of lawyer services vary widely and can be structured in different ways, either on hourly bases, flat fee bases, contingency bases (i.e., a percentage of what you receive), or a combination thereof. After discussing payment options with him, my entertainment lawyer, Rob Marcus, agreed to perform his services on my cable television network option and services agreement for a flat rate.

As for lawyers who are paid by the hour, Jim Arnoff explains, "If a lawyer is working for $250 an hour, [she'll] first need a retainer fee of $1,250. The retainer fee is the amount you pay before [the lawyer starts] services. The retainer isn't a prediction or estimate of the billing hours. If every single point gets negotiated, it will rack up hours. Your lawyer should keep you posted on the hours. A lawyer's hourly rate varies depending on his experience level and the law firm [she is] with. In New York City, this might be $350 an hour."

Beyond the Option

This author and the people interviewed for this book don't assume that it's possible to predict or diagnose every reader's legal needs in regards to negotiating a deal on a project. Besides, not all is equal among creators and their projects. Additionally, each network, Web destination, or production company has its own deal points it is willing to offer and others that it won't accept. A creator and his attorney's main concern is to make sure every important aspect of the deal is clearly defined. The goal is to have the creator attached to a project financially and creatively.

Contracts should lay out the long-term arrangement between both parties and define everyone's obligations and responsibilities on such milestones as the first, second, and third season of a series (obviously, a creator would like to see fees increase each year based on some percentage of the budget), as well as the creator's percentage of profits earned from ancillary merchandise. A creator's attorney will also try to keep his client attached to the project in the event that it spins off into a related area, such as direct-to-video features or theatrical features.

According to Rob Marcus, the list of potential negotiation points can go on and on depending on what's negotiated. He stresses the key issue that all points should be negotiated as part of the option agreement (or if in a separate agreement, then negotiated at the same time as and contingent upon the execution of the option agreement) because then, before the option is signed, is when the artist or owner will have the most leverage. And as Marcus explains in the quote that opens this chapter, "More often than not, the negotiation of a deal comes down to a single word: leverage."

Chapter 5

The Pitch Meeting Part I: The Creator's Corner

> "The biggest reason we conjure things for television is the audience. To hell with my creativity and to hell with the network executives, I serve the people who sit in front of the tube and want me to tell them a story. The executives and I [are] half in partnership and half in battle to deliver what we each think the audience wants."
>
> —**Doug TenNapel, creator of *Earthworm Jim* and *Catscratch***

Amen, brother TenNapel. This chapter's focus is on the pitch meeting, offering strategies, anecdotes, and dos and don'ts to help you and your project connect with a development executive. However, as TenNapel warns in his quote above, it's a mistake to create a pitch exclusively for the executives and their network. While it's true that you will be pitching to a development executive, the show you are pitching is for an audience. There are three factors that affect your project's chances of reaching that audience. First and foremost are the quality and merit of your pitch, which include how well you've made your case at the meeting and in the pitch bible. Second are the assets the creator brings to the table, based on industry reputation, prior achievements, and the quality of the relationship between the creator and the development executive. The third factor comprises all the elements out of the creator's control: the scope of the development executive's imagination, the development executive's personal taste, and the influence of current fads and trends and how they shape the needs of the network's development mandate.

It's easy to see how we could get swept up in the scramble to address all these factors. The good news is we don't have to, nor is it even possible to do so. A creator may score a development deal strictly from her reputation or relationship with a development executive. Another creator may have no prior relationship or known reputation but may have come in with a perfectly executed idea that was fully in harmony with that network's current development agenda. We can't hope to achieve the perfect balance. All we can do is take Mr. TenNapel's advice and think about our audience.

Setting Up a Pitch Meeting

Anyone with the ambition to create and pitch a show must first put a great amount of energy toward meeting development executives outside of a pitch meeting scenario. Relationship building is one of the key ingredients to a successful pitch, and it's better to have a healthy preexisting relationship with an executive than to just come in cold. If you live in New York City or Los Angeles, you have an advantage because it is possible to catch development executives at local industry events or even to set up informational meetings with them as a first contact. For those living elsewhere, phone calls can work nearly as well. In such a meeting or phone call, the development executive can explain what his company is looking for, which can save you and the executive valuable time before you set up a pitch meeting. It is always good to hear what the networks are buying now, but they routinely pick up projects outside that box for a variety of reasons, which is more reason to make a proposal that pleases you and your intended audience without getting too hung up on network mandates.

Fred Seibert, president and executive producer of Frederator, is especially generous with his time, often scheduling one or two meetings with brand new talent each week. If you're able to arrange such a meeting with a development executive, it is best to use that time to present yourself, find out what she is doing, and maybe show some samples of your work. In short, don't pitch at an informational meeting. This first meeting is just to establish trust and (hopefully) the foundation for a long-term

New York–area animation folks connect at the Platform International Animation Festival. Pictured left to right, starting with the back row, are Bill Plympton, Patrick Smith, Amid Amidi, the author, and Lisa LaBracio. Now, if I can just figure out who took my wallet. Photo from the author's collection.

relationship. A second meeting can be the one where you schedule a formal pitch, but never lose sight of the fact that each encounter, formal or informal, can help build a mutually beneficial relationship between you and the development executive. Some of my favorite people in the animation industry are development executives who have never green-lighted one of my projects. But the future is wide open with possibilities.

Another great way to meet development executives outside of a pitch meeting is to attend international animation festivals, such as Ottawa and Annecy, where there is always a strong network development presence. In a festival setting, everyone is there to schmooze, relax, and party. It's the perfect social atmosphere to make new contacts. After that, you can find gentle ways to stay in touch during the year without risking a restraining order. For more on this subject, see the chapter on networking in my book *Your Career in Animation: How to Survive and Thrive.* At festivals, do not attempt to pitch a project unless you've made an official appointment to do so. Mostly, these encounters should just be the foundation for building a relationship. Pulling out a pitch and catching an executive unawares is a good way to annoy a potential ally. Administering noogies is a similarly bad idea.

The most common question about development, after, "Will they steal my ideas?" (see chapter 4 on legal matters) has to be, "How do I set up a pitch meeting?" The answer is easy: you ask for one. Development executives are in the business of taking pitches. They can't do that without you and your ideas. So, all you have to do is get their contact info and request a meeting. Networks and their development executives can be searched online, and their contact info could be a few mouse clicks away. After reading a trade magazine article about a network dabbling in animation for the first time, I found a Web site that listed the network's general telephone number. The operator connected me to the development executive I'd read about, and from there it was easy to schedule a pitch.

You won't always get to meet with the development executive of your choice. Sometimes you might get pushed into taking a meeting with a lower level or junior executive. This is nothing to complain about, especially if you are fairly unestablished or new to pitching. It's possible that ten years down the line, this junior executive could be the top dog, single-handedly deciding "yay" or "nay." You need to have that big picture in mind and realize that every relationship has potential and should be treated with respect. Linda Simensky, vice president of children's programming at PBS, once told me that she remembers all the creators who were not interested in taking a meeting with her at the start of her development career. She still has a mental list of these names. Food for thought, I'd say.

On the flipside, several of the junior executives I've pitched to and formed great relationships with ended up leaving the industry. There's no guarantee that every seed you plant will flourish, but you might make a lifelong friendship or two along the way.

If you go the informational meeting route, don't leave without asking the executive lots of questions: What do they have in development that they're excited about now? What do they look for in a first pitch? Do they have any samples of good and bad pitch bibles you could see? What's the current development mandate or agenda of the network? Is it a bad idea to combine honey mustard and mayonnaise in a tuna salad? You get the idea.

The next logical question is, "Do I need an agent?" The answer is no, although some creators choose to use an agent. Typically, agents will not be interested in representing you if you're an unproven would-be creator, even though you may have years of experience in the animation industry. You are more desirable if you've already worked in a senior role on very visible projects. In that scenario, an agent may take a chance on you. Doug TenNapel adds, "Agents don't want to just set a meeting if they think you will lose their credibility in a room. There is a deep relationship between managers/agents and the studios, so the agency wants to protect its potency by knowing you're bringing in some magic to the pitch. The agency is on a first-name basis with all of the major studios and they say, 'Doug wants to show you something.' That's all it takes. Meeting set, and it's up to me to deliver a good pitch."

The best way to get an agent is to make her come to you. Your body of work, awards, and accomplishments should ideally have the agent discovering you and offering to be your representative. Although I have not yet produced a pilot for TV, my senior roles on several popular animated TV shows, my side career of writing books, and my leadership of ASIFA-East has led to my being approached by an agent. I opted not to take on an agent because of my existing relationships with most of the networks and their development executives.

Pitching Styles

There's an easy answer to finding your pitch style: be yourself. Like Brad Goodman says on *The Simpsons*, "There's no trick to it. It's just a simple trick."

I have a personal ritual I do just before a pitch meeting. I'm a pretty relaxed guy, but when I get a little nervous, my hands get a little clammy. My solution? I buy a 75-cent cup of coffee and I hold it. It warms my hand (and my soul), giving me a dry handshake and caffeinated confidence to face what's ahead.

Industry magazines and Web sites sporting articles on pitching often misinform us with macho tales of creators who nail pitches by working themselves up into a frothy frenzy. If this doesn't sound like you, don't try to go that route. Being the most energetic and exciting pitcher doesn't make your idea any better, nor does it guarantee the executive that you will be effective in helming a series and managing a crew. So, let's not overrate the importance of flashy pitching skills. In reality, a little sincerity and natural enthusiasm go a long way. Speaking of sincerity, never open your pitch by saying that you've got the best idea ever or that it's the next

SpongeBob. Statements like this raise skepticism. Just show them your idea. Give them a chance to draw an honest opinion. That's what you came for.

Before the pitch begins, the creator and executive try to figure out if they click as people. Most people liken it to dating, although I don't think it should be anywhere near as stressful as that. Whatever your pitching style is, don't forget to begin the meeting with a good, old-fashioned, getting-to-know-you chat. Both parties will want to talk about their backgrounds, and if the development executive neglects to do so, spur him on. He'll be glad to share because most everybody likes to talk about themselves. When the time comes to get down to business, the executive will give you the prompt to begin.

Doug TenNapel describes his pitching technique: "I keep the pitch short because length doesn't accomplish anything. I'll give the title (*KID BLAST!*) and a description of the type of show ('It's a puppet-animated action-comedy for boys six to eleven'). Then, I'll give a brief description of the show's content: 'It's about a kid and his gingerbread dog who just want to have a blast everywhere they go. You see, the kid and dog like to have fun, but the dog is made of cookie so they can't get him wet and bad guys want to eat him. By the end of each show, the dog is eaten or melted and Kid Blast just bakes up another batch of his favorite mutt.'"

Since animation is a visual medium, creators should be sure to display some pitch art on the table while they explain ideas like the one above. TenNapel reports that his next move is to present a paragraph description of the main characters, followed by three to five sample episode ideas. With that, the meeting can be done. He adds, "By this time, I'm already checking my watch and offering the executive an out in case the material just isn't for [her. Executives] usually have a few questions to feel out the material. It really isn't that hard of a decision at this point: either they get it and see dollar signs or [they] see it as something that will kill their career if they make it. Sometimes we go back to talking about movies or friends and families, or how interesting my artwork is in the pitch material, but essentially, a show has been pitched."

The Benefits of Not Over-Rehearsing

"You may think you have every question answered, which is good, but I can guarantee you they are going to ask you something you hadn't even thought of. Not that this is a bad

Butch Hartman's *The Fairly OddParents* (Frederator/Nickelodeon). Hartman is one of the rare breed of creator with more than one series to his name. Copyright 2008, Viacom International, Inc. All rights reserved.

thing. On the contrary, it actually adds to the collaborative process and makes the client feel involved."

—**Butch Hartman, creator of** *The Fairly OddParents* **and** *Danny Phantom* **(Nickelodeon)**

One of my favorite pitch experiences was pitching to Heather Kenyon and Alex Manugian during their time at Cartoon Network in Los Angeles. They are both a lot of fun to chat with, and we've enjoyed many times together at festivals around the world. The meeting went very well. I knew my project and was able to pitch it very naturally. Then, to my surprise, Heather and Alex asked a couple of questions on an area I had completely forgotten to talk about. My co-creator, Deborah M. Staab, and our co-developer, Allan Neuwirth, had asked these same questions (which concerned some main characters' motivations) during the creation of the pitch bible. And, here I was, forgetting to mention some of these key details! After I explained this missing piece of the puzzle, Kenyon and Manugian responded very well. It was a collaborative moment, much like Butch Hartman described above. I think my mistake helped connect them with the project, perhaps in a stronger way than if I'd pitched it perfectly on the first try. I've learned not to aim for perfection. It's not about delivering a perfect speech. As painter Bob Ross used to suggest, "We don't make mistakes; we just have happy little accidents."

Creator Etiquette and the Common Mistakes of Pitching

According to Linda Simensky, many people who pitch are either not that great at representing their property or don't seem to know it well enough to make the pitch sound completely enticing. Simensky advises, "Creators should know their properties and be able to talk about them, rather than reading from the pitch or doing an unfocused pitch that doesn't really represent the idea. Give examples of how a show is funny, rather than saying it's going to be funny."

Over many years of pitching, I have learned to pitch my projects with enthusiasm and spontaneity, and in the most concise manner I can. But I keep in mind that pitching is a two-way communication. You have to have an understanding for how the pitch is being received while you are giving it. You have to be ready and willing to be interrupted by questions and comments. Most of us need to hone our basic communication skills before we can focus on our pitching skills. A good form of practice is learning how to keep an audience engaged. Attend any industry panel discussion that opens the floor up to audience questions, and you'll see how much trouble the average person has expressing her thoughts or questions in a clear and concise manner. Holding the attention of development executives in a pitch meeting is important not just because they've made time to meet with you, but because if you can't capture and hold their imagination for one meeting, you can't expect your creation to capture an audience.

Linda Simensky, having received hundreds of pitches over the years, kindly offers a round-up of some of the mistakes that creators and producers make when pitching.

- When you are pitching to a network, know what shows it produces, and watch them before you come in. (You wouldn't interview for a job without knowing what the company does, would you?)

- Don't think that your show needs to be exactly like the other shows on the network. They have those shows already. Don't insist that you know a network better than its own executives, no matter how much you've studied. Maybe the network is trying to do something different.

- Don't tell the executive that other networks really like the idea and are interested. The pitching process is a lot like dating. If you wanted to date someone, would you tell that person how many other people are interested in dating you, or that you were interested in dating other people?

The Pitch Bible as a Leave-Behind

I'm always amazed at how much bad advice pops up on the subject of pitching animation. One recent online article advised readers to hand out copies of a pitch bible at the start of a meeting. In reality, that's a terrible idea. As soon as you hand over a pitch bible, the development executive has a choice whether to read ahead, become distracted, or not listen to you at all. A pitch meeting should not be a creator monologue either. There's a balance to strike. The creator should know his project but present it casually and conversationally, leaving lots of room open for questions and comments along the way. Save handing out pitch bibles until the end of the meeting. Don't even show that you have them until that moment. If you show your pitch bible, the development executive will ask for one, and you'll be stuck handing it over and fighting for her focus.

Going one step further, I know an entertainment lawyer who advises not even giving out pitch bibles at the conclusion of a meeting. He believes they should be mailed out after a meeting because this will help record that the meeting took place and that a pitch bible was received. These are two things that could come in handy in the unlikely event of a copyright dispute down the road. Instead of using a bible in the meeting, I advocate making three to six 10 × 14-inch color prints of show art that you can flip over one by one as you introduce and discuss the project.

After a pitch meeting, the pitch bible becomes a useful tool for the development executive because, if they're truly interested in your show,

Left: The pitch bible cover from Fran and Will Krause's *Gravy Train*, which led to a pilot called *The Upstate Four*. Lots of redevelopment occurs in a typical development deal, and a lot more can change than the name. *The Upstate Four*, its logo, and all related characters and elements are trademarks of and © 2008 The Cartoon Network.

Below: Show art from my pitch *Fiona Finds Out*.

the executives will have to sell it up the chain to the bosses above them. Cartoon Network's *Chowder* creator Carl H. Greenblatt adds, "They have to sell show ideas to their bosses to justify their jobs. The best ideas are the ones that they can pitch easily. Give them the tools to do that. Make their jobs easy for them."

Pitching with Partners

The good and the bad of developing and pitching shows with one or more partners is that it adds additional (and sometimes conflicting) voices to the creative process. Obviously, the right collaborators can make all the difference. By bringing in creative collaborators, the whole project has the potential to benefit from the talent, experience, relationships, and industry clout that each member brings to the table. I like that when I pitch with a partner there is somebody else there who might be able to field a question that gets by me. Besides, there is a supported feeling that comes from having an ally in the room.

Taking on creative partners is all the more important for newcomers to this industry. By teaming up with established artists and writers, outsiders can hone their ideas for presentation and serious consideration. The best pitches happen when the development executive is confident that the pitchers have the experience and ability to execute their vision. This is the whole point of a "creator-driven" show. An outsider has no proven ability to do this and no track record of having worked in the business in any capacity, so the experienced artist or writer adds credibility to the venture.

Not surprisingly, some established creators prefer to fly solo, at least when it comes to creating and pitching a project. Veteran creator Doug TenNapel explains, "While we're carving out what the show is going to be about, I'm in there as a creator, then I have a head writer, a director, a senior executive, and a junior executive. . . . I don't think we have enough chairs in the room for another partner."

Pitching: Phone/FedEx/Fax

Other forms of communication may play a role in pitching, too. I've only pitched once over the phone and I didn't enjoy the experience, nor do I think it best served my project. During a phone conversation, I couldn't

This is the story of five extraordinary 10 year olds dedicated to freeing children from the tyrannical rule of adults, especially parents. After all, it's parents that stop you from doing all the fun things in life like staying up all night, eating whatever you want, and building low orbit neutrino cannons that can level small cities in one blast. Parents are the ones who make you go to school, do chores around the house, and take piano lessons. Well, forget it. These kids have different plans. In the tradition of such teams as The Mighty Morphin Power Rangers and Dragonball Z, they have formed their own team called The Kids Next Door (but you can call them The KND) and they plan on doing things their way. They've declared war on adulthood and will die before they surrender. To mask their identity from nosey adults, they have taken numbers instead of names.

These are...THE KIDS NEXT DOOR:

Tom Warburton's series synopsis page from his pitch bible for Cartoon Network's *Codename: Kids Next Door.* I love the iconic characters on the left margin, which also help demonstrate the creator's mastery of numbers. *Codename: Kids Next Door*, its logo, and all related characters and elements are trademarks of and © 2008 The Cartoon Network.

read the room, so it was hard to tell how the pitch was being received. Unfortunately, not being there in person may also mean you don't have the development executive's complete attention. If you have to pitch over the phone, you should at least make sure to e-mail the development executives some show art that they can look at during the pitch. If I had to choose, I'd prefer to pitch through mailing or e-mailing a bible rather than pitching over the phone. This way, the pitch is self-contained and can be read and absorbed. Although for a first pitch on a project I would prefer to be in the room with the executive, sometimes you do what you have to do.

For a few first pitches I've flown to Los Angeles. The nice thing about getting on a plane in order to pitch is that it demonstrates a high level of sincerity on the creator's part. After any initial pitch, I follow up with revisions of those pitches by sending new materials through e-mail. Once the re-pitch has been reviewed, a phone call or conference call is set up to follow up and either get additional notes or the final word on a project. Another option is pitching via video conferencing, which is available to anyone with a high-speed Internet connection and access to instant messenger services. The sound and picture are close to real time, and the medium might even add a layer of comfortable removal or quirky awkwardness, which, under the right circumstances, could help your pitch.

The creator of Cartoon Network's *Codename: Kids Next Door*, Tom Warburton, scored quite a bit of pitching success—two pilots and one series—by sending pitches via overnight mail. Warburton scored his next two development deals (one for a book, the other for a new series pilot) by pitching in person. And Jackson Publick also pitched *The Venture Bros.* to Cartoon Network by mailing the development executive a pitch bible. Again, newcomers would be best advised to get an in-person meeting to first establish and introduce themselves. Tom Warburton and Jackson Publick each had the luxury of leaning on years of top-notch industry work experience and relationship building that, no doubt, served their mailed-in pitch proposals.

Pitching Extras

"For *The Powerpuff Girls*, my main selling point was my finished student film. I was able to pop in my film and actually show what I was talking about. After seeing the film, the development executive liked what she saw so much that she bypassed the rest of her development team and took me to see the president of the company, Fred Seibert. He watched it, liked what he saw, and started negotiations for *The Powerpuff Girls* that day."

—Craig McCracken, creator of *The Powerpuff Girls* and *Foster's Home for Imaginary Friends* (Cartoon Network)

As Craig McCracken's story shows, for some creators, pitch meeting extras make all the difference. This was especially so in this case because when McCracken sold *The Powerpuff Girls* he was a relatively unproven newcomer. It's true that nothing shows a creator's point of view or execution intent better than some finished animation. That said, there is an art to communicating execution within a pitch bible, and sometimes it may even be preferable for development executives to use their imaginations rather than be spoonfed a sneak preview of the final product. Test footage is a potentially lethal pitch extra, one that could taketh away as much as it giveth. In short, if your bit of finished animation is not TV perfect, don't show it. The production values should be top-notch and fully representative of how your show might look on-air.

Other pitch extras may include music/original songs or statues/maquettes of the characters. Stephen Hillenburg's pitch to Nickelodeon, featuring a yellow dude named SpongeBob SquarePants, utilized several pitch extras. Hillenburg recalls, "I created a bible and a few paintings to explain the characters and their world. To supplement this I sculpted SpongeBob, Patrick, and Squidward and put them in an aquarium where they were propelled by an air pump. I also recorded a temp theme song on a small tape recorder and mounted it inside a conch shell with a mercury switch so the song would play whenever the shell was lifted to the ear."

Butch Hartman advises creators to bring everything they think they'll need to answer the many questions of the people to whom they will be pitching, which might include written material, drawings, pictures, and videos—whatever it will take to get the point across. He says, "Remember, just because you've been living with an idea for a year or so doesn't mean that the client has. They are blank slates and you will have approximately ten minutes to fill their heads with just as much stuff as you have in yours."

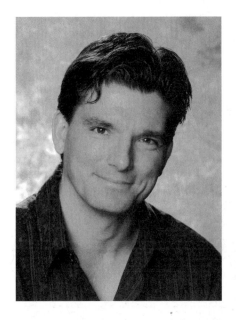

It's a bird! It's a plane! It's Butch Hartman! With two series already to his name, it seems only kryptonite can stop him now.

Each series pitch is unique, so each creator should figure out how pitch extras will best work in his or her pitch meeting. One rule is that the pitch extras should not be more interesting than the show itself. Use pitch extras to support the pitch, communicate a key aspect of the show, and help generate additional enthusiasm. You don't want to risk being gimmicky in your presentation. That could take away from the substance of your proposal and your credibility as a creator.

Pitching Buffet-Style at Industry Events

Newcomers to the world of pitching often find their best bet is to travel to annual industry events such as San Diego's Comic-Con, New York City's KidScreen Summit, Ottawa's Television Animation Conference (TAC), and France's MIPCOM. Despite the heavy price tag of airfare, hotel, and event admission, each of these events features designated pitch times where creators and executives sit down one-on-one for rounds of speed pitching that might last as long as fifteen minutes per meeting. Before you get too excited, consider this cautionary tale: A friend of mine who was an assistant to a well-known development executive at a top network told me that at the end of the event, the executive dumped all the pitches and business cards he accrued from the various creators right into the trash. There is a feeling among some development executives that they aren't

Show art from Doug Vitarelli's pitch, which he debuted at the KidScreen Summit in New York City. Image courtesy of the artist.

going to find series gold by sitting down to round after round of speed pitches open to the general public. Feeding this flame (or fantasy) is the rare outsider project, such as *Baby Einstein* (created by wife-and-husband team Julie Aigner-Clark and Bill Clark at their home in suburban Denver), which broke through to the big time, eventually transformed by Playhouse Disney into the hit TV series *Little Einsteins*.

For development executives, attending such events is more obligation than inspiration. The real opportunity it affords them is the chance to mingle, network, and conduct business with their own kind. Still, for the creator, any opportunity to pitch is good practice and experience.

Animator Doug Vitarelli describes his first experience in a round of five-minute speed pitching at the KidScreen Summit: "I had two meetings with network execs. The first guy told me that the last person had a great pitch (he had some animation and a toy) and that I had a lot to live up to. Bad vibes. My legs [were] cut out from under me. The wind had been taken from my sails. I spent two minutes babbling and then tried to recover, but I didn't. At the end he told me that my idea is not in the age range that he's looking for at the moment. I gave my next spot to someone else. I just wasn't going to waste my or another person's time right then." The next day, Vitarelli learned another key lesson in pitching. "The executive stopped me in the middle of my first sentence. 'What's your hook?' he asked. 'What's a hook?' was my reply. I found out a hook is a one- to two-sentence description that 'hooks' the person you're talking to. The conference had only five hours to go and I heard the word 'hook' three more times."

For better or worse, speed pitching allows a creator to pack years of the emotional roller coaster of pitching into mere minutes. The good news is that, for the creator, there is a lot more to these events than pitching. After the negative experience Doug Vitarelli describes above, he attended a lecture and Q&A with Craig Yoe, co-founder of YOE! Studio, which lifted his spirits and allowed him to feel much better about the intersection of art and commerce. Vitarelli adds, "The best place is just standing around while you're waiting for something. I was outside getting some fresh air and I struck up a conversation with a guy who [was] looking for an animator. He showed me his property, gave me a plush toy, and insisted that I get back in touch with him."

When asked whether the price of admission was worth it, Viterelli answers, "I would have to say it was. I really want my project to be a series and am willing to work hard and accept a few or many rejections because all I need is one person to greenlight it. I definitely need to do more—lots more—research for the next time I pitch. It's nice that I now have a huge database of names and e-mail addresses from the conference to help me."

The Waiting Game

> "If they don't love it immediately, you're in for a long,
> frustrating process."
> —Mo Willems, creator of *Sheep in the Big City* (Cartoon Network)

After the pitch meeting, how much time should a creator give a network to get back to him with a verdict? Most development executives or networks will tell you that it is their aim to give feedback on a pitch within two to six weeks, or even less. I can testify that sometimes this actually happens. More often, the wait can be as long as three months or more. From my experience, the longer waiting periods should not be blamed on the network; usually they are the result of an executive who is spread too thin and has myriad duties and responsibilities lying outside of development, and in some cases they are the result of the executive's inability to manage her own development process effectively. Whatever the reason, it leaves you waiting.

The next question, naturally, is, "Is it okay to show other networks my idea in the meantime?" The answer is absolutely "Yes!" In fact, you'd be a fool if you didn't. The fisherman with more lines in the water is more likely to get a nibble, right? The same applies here. The only time it would be a faux pas to do this is if a network asks you to hold off from showing the project to anybody else. If the executives do request this of you, make sure to agree on a set period of time you are willing to take the pitch out of further circulation. In all fairness, this is the purpose of an option payment by the network, in which the network pays a flat fee to reserve its option to buy the property at a later time. Still, It's okay to give a network, should they request it, a two-week grace period before continuing to pitch a project. The far more likely scenario is that networks will assume you are pitching elsewhere simultaneously. Make sure you are not pushing your simultaneous pitching in each network's face. It is a mistake to try to play networks against each other. If you are in the enviable position of having two networks interested in your property at the same time, your lawyer or representative, under your counsel, should negotiate the better all-around deal.

If you find yourself waiting longer than one month for feedback, it is okay to gently check in with the executives. I like to shoot them an e-mail asking them if they've had a chance to review the materials and if they can offer any feedback. If the waiting period extends into the three months or more, I might check in with a call or e-mail every couple of months, sometimes not even asking about the project, but just saying, "Hello," or giving them some news about a personal film project I'm working on, or simply to tell them how much I'm enjoying a new show on their network. These unobtrusive check-ins remind the executives you are still out there and help sustain the relationship, while giving them a very gentle nudge for feedback.

Once the wait for an answer exceeds three months, it might be best to consider that you did, in fact, get an answer: No. It's a shame that it has to work that way, but that is sometimes the reality. The good news is that you weren't just waiting on one network's answer. You pitched several places at once. This should help even the most obsessive among us to let it go and move on. Never take the news (or non-news) personally.

As much as writing is rewriting, pitching is re-pitching and development is redevelopment. Tack ten years on to that and you'll see how much time and effort it took for me to make my first deal. It requires a thick skin to keep truckin' down the (probably very long) road toward a deal. Still, it is hard to imagine a better reward.

Chapter 6

The Pitch Meeting Part II: The Money Side of the Table

"I used to joke that I was renaming the pitching process 'come in and tell us about your idea' so it would sound less stressful. But the nature of the process is that it is stressful."
—**Linda Simensky, vice president of children's programming, PBS**

My friend, mentor, and fellow Beatlemaniac Linda Simensky (also vice president of children's programming at PBS).

Linda Simensky and I recently enjoyed a nice lunch during which she told me that she wished more development executives realized that the creators hold the real power, despite the god-like role that the development executive seems to play in the pitching process. In truth, the development executive needs the creator, her idea, and her unique vision to execute the project to a successful finish. At the risk of coming across as overly diplomatic, I suggest that the real power lies not exclusively with the creator or the development executive or network. The real power is in the combination of the two and how the winning relationship can develop and distribute something successful that brings mutual creative satisfaction as well as financial success.

Network Development Executives Are People, Too

If I were a Jane Goodall–type assigned to live amongst the development executives, I'd probably find them to be very interesting creatures. No, they don't eat their young or fling feces if cornered, but they do wear many hats: they are gatekeepers, communicators of the network development mandate, talent scouts, visionaries, and cheerleaders. Most important, network development executives are your potential partners. Should your wacky idea about mushrooms from outer space sell, they're the ones who will guide you to the finish line. The good news is that they need you as much as you need them. They can't create a series without you. At this point you may be asking where this unique species, the development executive, originates.

Linda Simensky answers, "You'll find that every development executive has a different background, although most are probably interested in creative areas or studied liberal arts in college. Most do not have backgrounds in animation but have a genuine interest in storytelling or humor or other creative areas. Most network development executives start out in entry-level jobs at the network and work their way over."

Alice Cahn, vice president of social responsibility at Cartoon Network, feels that there are some common experiences a development executive must have: "These include, but are certainly not limited to, working with or otherwise acquiring in-depth knowledge of the target audience for whom you are developing projects; appreciating the properties of the media for which you are developing; and understanding the larger environment within which your project will exist. These sets of experiences could come from having spent time working in media, in education, in business, in the arts world, at home raising kids, or some combination."

Eric Coleman, senior vice president of development at Walt Disney

Television, knows executives who were previously teachers, writers, lawyers, or wandering backpackers (that was him). "It's hard to break in, but once you get your foot in the door you need to develop a number of qualities: a good eye for talent, an ability to inspire, nurture, and collaborate with this talent, and a passion for both the creative content and its intended audience. Developing a project takes years so you really have to enjoy the process itself, not just the part where the series gets on air and it's a big hit. Especially since they're not all big hits."

The Juggling Game

What does a development executive do outside of the pitch room? No, this is not the setup to a dirty joke. You should be ashamed of yourself for even thinking that. Contrary to popular misconceptions, development executives don't spend their days trying to find creative ways to avoid getting back to you with an answer on your pitch. In fact, taking and responding to pitches is only a small part of a development executive's day-to-day job. This is no different at PBS, where Linda Simensky says there is no member of the kids' programming department who handles only development. She continues, "We oversee all of kids programming, so we handle program strategy and scheduling, development, and current series. In addition, we work closely with other departments, so we are involved with interactive, marketing and branding, business affairs, and several aspects of management at different levels. We speak at and arrange a number of meetings each year with the PBS stations, as well."

Responsibilities to current series are often a natural outgrowth of a development executive's role on the development of that series, and

Teletoon's manager of original production, Athena Georgaklis, who squeezed in an interview with this author during a busy week at the KidScreen Summit. Never underestimate the power of coffee and pie!

sometimes allow the executive to continue as the executive in charge of production. Teletoon's manager of original production, Athena Georgaklis, oversees four or five series at once. She also has a number of shows in development and manages the production slate to make sure everything comes in on time. Georgaklis says, "Because we're a network we work with a whole bunch of different departments, such as marketing, and make sure that the flow of info goes from our office in Montreal to the director in Toronto and to everyone else. We work on a lot of material here that will not be seen by anyone else for eighteen months, so it's really important that we're communicating what we're doing to the rest of the team and to the rest of the network so that they can get behind what's coming."

While at Cartoon Network, development executive Heather Kenyon found that a huge aspect of her job was to find talent. She says, "You can't wait for the perfect pitch to walk through the door. We meet with agents but also attend film festivals, screenings, art gallery openings, check out what is new at comic book stores, read graphic novels, speak at events and schools, watch graduation and short films, read blogs, watch YouTube, and visit random Web sites. This is a facet of development and it is never finished. There is always another rock to turn over to try and find that next big thing."

Nickelodeon's president of animation, Brown Johnson, explains that managing difficult creators is also a development executive's responsibility. Johnson explains, "I find there is a little 'crazy' in all creative people. Mostly good crazy. Sometimes creators take a lot of handling because some of them think they can do everything on a show (write, direct, and produce), but I have never met one person who could do all of that effectively. Development executives need to build strong teams around creators to ensure a series is on time, on budget, and creatively successful."

On my recent TV directing job, Adult Swim's *Assy McGee*, the executive in charge was Cartoon Network's Matt Harrigan, who also juggled head writing and producing roles on our series, in addition to similar roles on other Adult Swim shows under his supervision. If it sounds like Harrigan is already spread thin, he also takes pitches and shepherds pilots and series through development. Creators staring at their iPhones, waiting for word on pitches, might do well to consider all the duties a development executive takes on every day.

First Encounters of the Best Kind

A hard part of the development executives' job is frequently saying, "No." Most of what comes their way does not fit what they are looking for, or (gasp!) is simply not very good. For a first pitch to be of maximum use to development executive and creator alike, it's best to pitch the idea relatively early instead of slaving away on it for months or years in attempts to make the perfect pitch package. Linda Simensky agrees, "I prefer to see something at the very beginning, and at this point, I can tell people if the idea is interesting and a good fit for us. Then, they can go back with some feedback and develop it a little more fully for us specifically." Of course, a creator should still know his project inside out, even when showing it early in its development.

Realistically, creators should keep in mind that once they bring back their redeveloped projects, there is still no guarantee that the network will go for them. This does not make this method a waste of time. All creative time spent on self-initiated projects is time well spent. By coming back with a retooled pitch, the creator has the opportunity to address whatever notes might help take the project toward the next level. If the second pitch fails to make the sale, one network's feedback might help you make the sale to one of their competitors. Pretty sneaky, eh?

Most development executives assume that it might take a few tries before a project is ready to be picked up. Linda Simensky affirms, "We have looked at many projects at several different stages. I can think of several projects that came to us that weren't what we were looking for, but after numerous discussions and changes, a few have ended up in our commissioning rounds. I think it is rare for an idea to come in fully figured out and fitting perfectly into our lineup. Everything usually requires some feedback."

However, Simensky suggests that if a project isn't working after a few tries, it's usually best to move on. In some cases, I've encountered development executives who flat-out refuse to see a project pitched a second time. In their eyes, if they saw it once and didn't buy it, then it's a pass. There are instances in which that's justified, but in some cases it means the executive is only interested in the bottom line, not in building relationships or nurturing talent.

There's yet another reason to pitch a project in its early development. If a first pitch is presented in a thick, polished pitch book with all the trimmings, the development executive can assume the creator won't be open to feedback. Development executives like to see solid ideas that leave some room for their input. A first meeting should begin a discussion—a free exchange of feedback and ideas from both sides of the table.

Ideally, a creator will pitch two or three ideas at once, all in the early development (two-sheet) stage. Heather Kenyon says, "If I am just getting to know a creator or [creators] are just getting to know our network, I like it when they come in with two or three pitches that they can go through and discuss. By discussing the pitches and what works for our network and what doesn't, we can both get a better idea of each other's sensibilities."

Development Executive Etiquette and the Common Mistakes of Taking Pitches

In my first book's chapter on pitching and development, I was able to exorcise the trauma of my encounter with a worst-case scenario development executive. My story documented the rise and fall of a development deal in which a network tried to engage my services to revive and redevelop a classic cartoon property. In short, this opportunity imploded when it became clear that the executive's style of management was adversarial. Instead of protecting me and preserving my trust, he used our every encounter to browbeat me and remind me that I was, in his words, "below the radar," which was his way of saying, "Just sign the damn contract." Over the course of an unhappy year spent negotiating and renegotiating this deal, my enthusiasm waned and my desire to do the project could not compete with my urge to flee and wash my hands of the whole mess.

This sad affair didn't sour me on development or development executives. Instead, I learned the important lesson that development executives are half of the development relationship, and if that relationship is unhealthy, the project will suffer or, as in my case, never get off the ground. I'm not the only one to learn from this experience. Years later, an industry insider confessed that he heard the executive express deep regret over his behavior during his time at the network, blaming it on the influence of a bad mentor. More development executives would be wise to treat everyone ("below the radar" or not) with professional respect and common courtesy. Not all of these eager, young, would-be creators are going to disappear. Some of them might go on to create the next *Dora the Explorer* or *South Park*, or at the very least, write a tell-all book about their experiences. Maybe the next *Mommie Dearest* will be about an animation development executive.

I think the worst thing a development executive can do is to give a creator reason to not trust her. On two occasions, different development executives have told me that my project was going forward and then reneged on their word. I'm not suggesting they were lying when they first told me the good news, but they may have spoken prematurely before the answer was truly locked in place. Another time, a development manager withheld important creative information through the development of a project. At each stage, this individual played games like asking for opinions from the creative team after a different plan, which would be revealed afterwards, was already put into motion. Animation development is a collaborative art and it is real shame for either a development executive or a creator to behave in a way that is counterproductive to a project's success. Some see a creator's stories of bad experiences dealing with executives as proof of a flawed development system. But bad development executives don't represent an entire group of people, or the development system everywhere.

Linda Simensky, having provided us with a handy creator etiquette list in the previous chapter, generously offers a list of the common mistakes development executives may make while taking a pitch.

- Not being honest. It is hard to say no, but I think most people would rather have an honest answer than think the pitch was great and then get rejected.

- Acting too self-important. Someday, you might be on the other side of the desk, pitching to this person.

- Being curt. Sometimes, the pitch you are looking at isn't one you fall in love with, but perhaps this creator will be back with something better next time. Offer feedback and/or encouragement, rather than just some terse comments.

The Truth Behind Network Mandates

Ask a development executive to tell you what they are looking for and they'll likely refer you to their network's current development mandate.

A still from Janet Perlman's Cartoon Network pilot, *Penguins Behind Bars*, which ran afoul of the network's changing development mandate upon completion. The ground often moves under one's feet in this business, which is one more reason to reign in one's expectations. *Penguins Behind Bars*, its logo, and all related characters and elements are trademarks of and © 2008 The Cartoon Network.

On paper, the mandate is a neat and tidy, creative call to arms, clearly asking for shows that skew toward boy or girl, older or younger, action or comedy, etc. Such statements are usually a result of committees in conference rooms and are based on marketing reports that chart fads and trends while trying to predict what might be popular two years from now. Development mandates are far from an exact science. Whatever is greenlighted for production today may not appear on air for another two years. Athena Georgaklis explains, "Since our next shows won't hit the air for at least another year and a half, we're always thinking ahead: 'What will be the next trend?' We might be more girl skewed one year and then we could decide, 'Okay, that really didn't work.' So, we'll add some more boy stuff into the mix or skew older perhaps."

Newer platforms, such as broadband Internet channels, are changing the equation and drastically cutting down the time it might take from greenlight to broadcast. Will this result in shows more correctly gauged to match to a current audiences' taste? Time has yet to tell. Keeping up with trends is not necessarily any easier than predicting how trends will change years from now, nor does it guarantee a good show. Remember, if analyzing marketing reports led to hit shows, wouldn't all shows be successful? Wouldn't the networks be batting a thousand?

Creators would be wise to use the network creative mandates and development memos as a way of figuring out what the buyers are looking for. Maybe your idea fits within this box and maybe it doesn't, or maybe it will next year. In short, don't worry too much about it. Athena Georgaklis explains, "It's not black and white. At the end of the day, we're all still trying to figure it out. It would help both the executives and the creators to know, 'This is the exact direction we're taking right now, excluding everything else.' But the problem is everyone is afraid that they'll miss the next big idea." Linda Simensky adds, "I always get the sense that creators and producers feel that we are holding information back—that we know the answers or we know exactly what we are looking for and we're just not sharing it." Development executive Peter Gal, speaking on a development panel at the Platform International Animation Festival, confessed that he tried to seriously follow the network's annual development mandate, but found that interesting pitches always came from outside those parameters, pushing the network in unexpected directions.

Another use of development mandates might be to provide a ready and convenient excuse to reject unsuitable pitches, sometimes coming from untested or unknown talent. However, the development mandate is helpful to newcomer creators in that it allows them (at least superficially) a peek inside the network's thought process and business plan—for whatever that's worth.

The Effects of Fads and Trends

Pitch even once and you are likely to encounter the very real consequence of current fads and trends or the predicted fads and trends of the near future. While all shows are products of their day and age, hit shows that are able to stand the test of time will not be based on hot new trends, fads, or technology. While they may include some of those elements, they will not *be* the element. However small a role they should play, there's no denying that fads and trends weigh into the development process. Fads and trends might be derived from a new pop band, fashion, technology such as iPods, or even from other animated shows that rival networks may try to match in tone, style, or subject.

Brown Johnson states that today's audience, no matter how old, has a huge appetite for *new*. Her answer at Nickelodeon is to try to channel what is new into something that is unique, playful, and authentic while showing respect for the audience. Similarly, Linda Simensky says, "As far as trends go, PBS Kids has always been more interested in creating trends than following them."

Compelling characters are the essential ingredient in any project. A creator would be wise to keep the emphasis on character rather than pander to the shifting wind of fads and trends. Heather Kenyon says, "Yes, we would keep tabs on how kids are feeling and thinking to make sure that our programming responded to their needs, but we didn't pay too much attention to what [was] selling at the mall. By the time a new show hits the air, Crocs will be a distant memory. Remember? They are those shoes . . . plastic . . . bright colors . . . they slip on . . ."

The Influence of New Media Platforms on the Development Process

Nobody can deny that the viewing public is now dividing its time between TV and online destinations. This message has not been lost on the pay TV and broadcast TV networks, which have their own online presence. For example, AtomFilms.com is the online arm of MTV Networks, and SuperDeluxe.com performs the same function for Cartoon Network's Adult Swim. As Atom Films vice president of acquisitions and production Megan O'Neill says, online development is cheaper and faster. Best of all, these online divisions of the major networks allow for greater risk taking, enabling edgier projects to break through—perhaps all the way back to a place on the TV screen.

Linda Simensky reports that at PBS Kids, new platforms have already changed the development process from creating series to creating multi-platform properties. She explains, "Certainly now there are more opportunities to get ideas seen in other media, and more opportunities to get experience." PBS Kids puts its money where its mouth is by requiring creators to include potential Web crossover ideas in their pitch proposals.

At the present time, online destinations are making their biggest impact on the network development process by acting as virtual ap-

Megan O'Neill, vice president, acquisitions and production, Atom Films. O'Neill's former film distribution company (with co-founder Harold Warren), Forefront Films, represented my first film, *Snow Business* (1998).

plause meters and charting viewing habits, tastes, and viral popularity. A high-ranking clip on YouTube might attract a TV development executive to contact its creator, perhaps leading to a development deal, pilot, or series. Development executives are aided in their search through links discovered by their friends, families, colleagues, and also officially by production assistants and interns. *Making Fiends*, a series created by Amy Winfrey, ran first as a self-produced online series (2003–2006), before transforming into a Nickelodeon series that first aired in 2008. Certainly more examples of the same are out there and even more will follow as the years roll by.

Web destinations, such as SuperDeluxe.com and AtomFilms.com (owned by Turner and MTV Networks, respectively), acquire existing short films and seek original content, which they can produce, own, and post on their sites. The parent companies ensure that this low-risk development could spin into a TV series similar to the way that the original *Beavis & Butt-Head* and *South Park* independent shorts led to successful series.

An interesting side effect of original development at such venues as Super Deluxe and Atom Films is the need for short (under three minutes), funny, and adult-oriented content. In this development model, contracts come together more quickly and more often, so creators may benefit from pitching their wares via less conventional means than the pitch bible. These online destinations are looking for ready projects that won't require lengthy periods of traditional network paper development. Megan O'Neill advises that would-be pitchers to Atom first create a short trailer or the first episode. She says, "I have funded several animated properties, including Aardman's new series *Pib and Pog*, based on a short film. We acquired *Pib and Pog* several years ago, and when Aardman pitched a new series of episodes, it was easy to say yes. We already knew the characters, the quality of work, etc."

A still from PES's award-winning short, *Game Over*, which was pitched over the phone to Megan O'Neill at Atom Films. Creator's chances for success are much greater if they are already established in the industry. Image courtesy of Atom Films and PES.

In the short format of online content, even an original song might be enough to secure a greenlight. Megan O'Neill notes that Atom Films pre-bought a Flash short called "I Can't Afford My Gasoline," based on the creator singing the song to her over the phone. "We had had success with several of Dominic Tocci's other pieces, and when he sang the song to me, it just cracked me up." This looseness is not matched in network development. Megan O'Neill summarizes, "It's difficult to get a show on network or cable TV, especially [for] young creators who may only have one or two shorts under their belt. While the dollars are much smaller online, you can have lots of creative freedom. Once we say yes to a project, you aren't stuck in development hell for years. You have the ability to create the episodes, and once we put it up, you get quite a lot of feedback from your audience online. It's a great test of the characters and storyline."

Other Development Models

There are other development models out there that may vary from network to network or change from year to year. For a brief period in the 1990s,

Nickelodeon had a creative lab department whose only function was to develop and produce unique short-form animation and live action that could be aired as interstitials (shorts airing among or between regular-length series) while at the same time providing a means to discover and develop new talent. If you hear of something similar currently going on, run—don't walk. These windows of opportunity don't stay open very long.

Nick Jr. is known throughout the industry for its own unique approach to development, mostly doing paper development based on specific assignments. "One year it might be a math show, or music another year. We reach out to familiar creators or production companies or to new creators whose work has inspired us," says Nickelodeon animation president Brown Johnson.

In fact, Nick Jr. has two versions of creative assignments: short-form and long-form. The most recent short-form assignments were for projects featuring a strong father-figure theme. A two-page sheet outlined the creative parameters, submission format, and deadline. This is a fairly open call that includes a pretty broad base of creators, many of whom might be first-timers. Nick Jr. doesn't pay for the initial pitch proposals, but if chosen, the creator will get to make a short or interstitial, hence the term short-form development. These interstitials air in-between series programs and may serve as an unconventional series pilot. Brown Johnson points out, "Both *Wonder Pets!* and *Ni Hao, Kai-Lan* were shorts before going to series."

Nick Jr.'s long-form development begins each year with a specific mandate as well, as Brown Johnson explained above. The difference here

Character art from my pitch to Nick Jr., tailored to the network's short-form development mandate.

ULTRA

THE
**METH
MINUTE** 39

Ultra from an episode of *The Meth Minute 39* (Frederator), a groundbreaking online series featuring thirty-nine stand-alone shorts from the mind of creator Dan Meth. Image courtesy of Frederator.

is that Nick Jr. often acts as matchmaker, pairing experienced writers with seasoned animation directors, for instance. Each pair works on its pitch under paid contract. Once all teams submit their proposals, Nick Jr. chooses which may go to pilot, often choosing more than one project to move forward. Down the road, the completed pilots vie against one another for a series pick-up.

Another form of development is shorts programs, such as the Frederator/Nickelodeon *Random! Cartoons* shorts program featured in chapter 7. Similar shorts programs exist at Cartoon Network (*Cartoonstitute*) and The Disney Channel (*Shorty McShorts' Shorts*). Again, when a shorts program is initiated, run (don't walk) to participate. These windows close and programs fill up quickly. Frederator filled its thirty-nine seven-minute short slots in under one year's time. Short programs tend to have their own creative agenda, which may differ from their network counterparts. Be sure to find out the creative direction of the program you want to pitch. The primary goal of shorts programs is to make a bunch of stand-alone cartoons in hopes that something may stick.

A major drawback of the shorts programs for networks is the great expense they undertake to fully execute so many pilot films at once, resulting in only one or two cartoons moving forward to series. Perhaps the future of this model of development will live in a faster and less expensive form online. Frederator recently completed thirty-nine independently produced and funded stand-alone original Web cartoons called *The Meth Minute 39*, all created by animator Dan Meth. Before the films were even complete, one of them, *Night Fite,* had already spun off into its own commercially sponsored Web series. In a similar vein, Twentieth Century Fox recently established an in-house animation department for the first time in its history for the purpose of creating low-cost, short-form, animated Web content with the hope that something might become its next *Family Guy*–sized hit.

Amid Amidi, on his informative CartoonBrew.com Web site (which he heads with co-brewmaster, Jerry Beck) suggests one other development model that has yet to be tried. "I've long felt that development programs today are shortsighted by focusing on the creation of one-hit wonders and trendy properties, instead of pouring their resources into the long-term development and nurturing of talented artists, who in turn could develop many successful properties."

Amidi's suggestion mirrors how hit cartoon characters were hatched and nurtured to superstardom in the old days of the theatrical short. Back then, cartoons were a pre-sold part of the moviegoing package that also included newsreels, a main feature, a B-feature, and even live-action short subjects. Over the span of decades, animation crews at such studios as MGM, Warner Brothers, and Walter Lantz Productions had the opportunity to master their craft and develop star characters. Today's shorts programs are a mere shadow of the creative incubator that existed naturally in the business model of 1930s, '40s, and '50s cartoon-making. Given the amount of money major media companies and networks are willing to spend (or waste) each year, it's not impossible to imagine that one of these days someone will have the hindsight to re-implement what worked for yesterday's animation development.

However, it's important to note that the so-called golden age of animation was not so golden when it came to the creator's wallet. For instance, William Hanna and Joseph Barbera created the star cartoon characters Tom and Jerry while employed by Metro-Goldwyn-Mayer's animation studio. Typical of that period, the big studio made all the riches and the creators were paid a salary, never to share in the millions of dollars their creations helped to generate.

In a Perfect World

After all is said and done, can we conclude that the process by which networks take pitches and develop shows is fatally flawed? The answer

Development executive Heather Kenyon surrounded by animation artists at a New York City pub. From left to right: Justin Simonich, Xeth Feinberg, the author (moving too fast for the camera), Heather Kenyon, and Will Krause. The creator's and the executive's sides of the table need not be so far apart, especially when alcohol is involved. Photo by Richard O'Connor.

largely depends on who you ask, although it may surprise you that none of the executives interviewed for this book had any trouble naming the frustrating flaws in development for both executives and creators alike. Remember, much like an animator is hired to animate to set of specific instructions, so is a development executive hired to work within a network's guidelines and to find and help develop shows that suit its creative mandate and business model. Development executives are not hired to be activists and turn a whole system on its ear.

Animation artists and writers certainly have their opinions on what is wrong in the world of development, and have had no trouble expressing themselves on message boards and personal blogs. It might surprise some animation artists to learn that development executives are aware of the frustrations and complaints. All the development executives I've interviewed wished they could give answers on pitches sooner as well as speed up the deal negotiation on projects they choose to develop.

I understand all the criticisms and agree with many of them, but I choose not to focus on the negative. As creators, we should expect that there will always be problems or flaws in the development system, much as there will always be good and bad development executives. Our concerns are only to create with sincerity and sell our projects as smartly as possible, while filtering out all the factors beyond our control.

Chapter 7

Emotional Rescue

"Our experiences together are really instructive, and you've obviously succeeded in every way without anything from me."
—Fred Seibert, president and executive producer, Frederator

I first told Fred Seibert about this book in 2007 during one of our lunches in Manhattan. Fred joked that I should include a whole chapter on him. Well, a good idea is a good idea. My publisher and I had already decided to include a chapter covering the emotional roller coaster inherent in the pitching and development process. The more stock I took of my own pitching and development history, the more I realized my biggest highs and lows (and most important lessons learned) all involved Mr. Fred Seibert. I have always been and will remain in awe of Fred's accomplishments and influence in this industry. He is single-handedly responsible for giving dozens of animation artists the opportunity to make their own creator-driven shorts. These creators have ranged from fresh, previously untested talent (Pendleton Ward) to seasoned industry professionals (John R. Dilworth and Doug TenNapel).

If you read about my experience and believe that it only represents myself, my projects, Fred, and the exact moments in time presented here, then you're making a big mistake. Chances are, if you've already had some experience in pitching and development, you'll see shades of your story here too.

Some of my original pitch art for *Tad and His Dad*, co-created with Rich Gorey, which inadvertently became a great case study of the pitfalls in development.

The Godfather of the Creator-Driven Era

Once upon a time, in the not-too-distant 1980s, the TV animation landscape was still dominated by the Saturday morning cartoons of the three big networks. I was one of the little kids who shot out of bed every Saturday morning to watch shows that were often based on a line of toys. Don't judge me. We didn't have a lot of choices back then. One of my fondest memories is making pancakes with my dad so that they'd be ready in time to sit down to Filmation's *Tarzan, Lord of the Jungle* series. My Dad, a lifelong Tarzan fan, enjoyed the cartoon even more than I did. Today's mega-hits, such as *South Park*, *Blue's Clues*, and *Family Guy,* all have ancillary merchandise, but the difference is that the shows now drive the toys. Most agree that the modern age of cartoons begins in the late '80s with the release of *An American Tail* (1986), *Who Framed Roger Rabbit?* (1988), Disney's return to form with *The Little Mermaid* (1989), and the birth of *The Simpsons* (1989).

Yet, it can be argued that the main catalyst in the emergence of the creator-driven cartoon era belongs to the actions of one man: Fred Seibert. After picking the brains of several of animation's living legends from the golden age of the Hollywood cartoon, Fred devised the idea to let animators loose to make pilots that would somewhat resemble the way theatrical shorts were created in the golden age (roughly from 1928 through the 1940s). Fred's first move in this direction was as a consultant in the late

'80s, helping Nickelodeon make the leap into original programming for the first time in its history. Loosely following his advice, Nickelodeon executives implemented a plan under which they discovered and helped develop *The Ren & Stimpy Show*, *Rugrats*, and *Doug*. Not a bad start.

"I wanted to create short, seven-minute, funny cartoons with vivid characters and hilarious stories and gags the way the great cartoonists of the '30s and '40s did it," Fred recalls. "A lot of industry professionals thought I was crazy." The key difference between Fred's plan and the way it had been enacted by Nickelodeon was that he had intended to produce a larger number of pilots, at a standard length, with the intention of airing each one in an anthology-style series. In contrast, Nickelodeon made relatively few pilots at varying lengths, none of which was intended for broadcast. In the Nickelodeon model, pilots were made for boardroom meetings and focus-group testing, not for general audience consumption. Fred's plan was to throw dozens of original cartoon pilots at the wall to see which ones might stick, and with the hope that the viewing audience would help decide.

Fred found the opportunity to try creator-driven cartoons his way when he became president of Hanna-Barbera in 1992 and initiated the *What A Cartoon!* program, an anthology series made up of creator-driven, stand-alone shorts. He states in his official biography: "That grand experiment gave us forty-eight original shorts, an Academy Award nomination, two Emmy nominations, and seven original half-hour cartoon series (*The Powerpuff Girls*, *Johnny Bravo*, *Cow and Chicken*, *I Am Weasel*, *Courage The Cowardly Dog*, *Dexter's Laboratory*, and *What A Cartoon!*)." This was followed by a stint at Nickelodeon, where he used the same techniques to produce *Oh Yeah! Cartoons*, an anthology series of the same vein. "Now renamed *Random! Cartoons*, it features the work of some of the most talented professionals in cartoons today," Seibert says. "This anthology series gave kids ninety-nine different cartoons, including *The Fairly OddParents*, *ChalkZone*, and *My Life as a Teenage Robot*."

Seibert's development plan helped discover and nurture many of the creators piloting cartoons forward to this day. Recent shorts development initiatives from Cartoon Network, The Disney Channel, and Twentieth Century Fox show the continued commitment across the network boundaries to produce original, creator-driven, short cartoons. Seibert's "crazy" plan has cast a long shadow.

Me and Fred and a Dog Named Blue

One day in 2003, I came upon a massive, two-part interview with Fred Seibert conducted by Joe Strike for AWN.com. I printed it out and it became my companion on the subway train for the next few days. Some months later, the New York City chapter of Women in Animation presented an evening with Fred Seibert. Thankfully, not being a woman proved no obstacle to my attendance at the event, and I went with a few friends from Nickelodeon. I was disarmed by what I saw. Fred sat on a cushy armchair, drinking tea and discussing his career. Recently, I'd had a pitch rejected by a network that didn't want another animal show featuring the same animals as a show already in production. Incidentally, when that network show finally emerged two years later, it bombed and bit the dust hard. Fred seemed to speak to this network attitude, saying, "I don't mind looking at your idea about a bunny even though there is already Bugs Bunny out there. Your bunny might be different. There's room for more bunnies." Listening to Fred, I began to feel like the Beatles might have felt at the foot of the Maharishi Mahesh Yogi. Had I found my development-world guru?

A nice feature of Women in Animation events is that everyone in the audience is asked to quickly introduce herself at the start of the evening. I noticed Fred perk up when I labeled myself a *Blue's Clues* animation director. When question-and-answer time arrived I tried to make a further

Fred Seibert and the author chat before an ASIFA-East event celebrating Frederator's original Web series, *The Meth Minute 39*, created by Dan Meth. Photo courtesy of Frederator.

impression upon him by asking, "Don't you think that networks often learn the wrong lesson [about] why shows are successful?"

"No," Fred responded.

This simple exchange reflected the relationship that was to follow: me wanting Fred's approval (or greenlight) and him saying, "No." I made it a point to speak to Fred after the event, especially after he mentioned his latest project, a series of animator-created children's books made for Nick Jr. The books would act as low-cost preschool pilots, testing out characters and creators in hopes of finding a potential TV series in the mix. I loitered after the event until I had a chance to express my interest in pitching some children's books to Fred.

First Time at Bat

By early 2004, I had already illustrated more than a dozen *Blue's Clues* books for such publishers as Golden Books, Scholastic, and Simon & Schuster. Best of all, I had two solid preschool ideas ready to go, which I'd developed as animation pitches and could now be used as stand-alone manuscripts for children's books. Only days after I first met Fred, we had our next meeting in my *Blue's Clues* office at Nickelodeon. Unfortunately, Fred was not interested in my pitches. He felt that they were too concept-based. One idea focused on a character who wanted to grow up before her time. The second idea was about a new student dealing with the first day in a new school.

Fred wanted characters, period. He cited *Curious George* as the best example he could think of. "Curious George is a great character because he can go anywhere and the stories come from him. His curiosity creates the stories," he explained.

At this meeting, I learned Fred's signature business practice of never officially saying, "No." Unlike some network development executives, Fred is open to seeing your idea again and again if you're willing to keep working on it. Of course, Fred's lack of an official "no" is far from a "yes," but at least it keeps the conversation alive. Next Fred uttered something I would hear him say many times thereafter in the upcoming years: "I could be wrong. I'm wrong 99 percent of the time." In saying this, Fred admits he knows he could be passing on the next *Dora the Explorer*.

At the end of the meeting, Fred encouraged me to try again.

A month later I wrote a third script, this time for an older preschool

A still from my new short, *Owl and Rabbit Play Checkers,* which evolved out of my pitch of the same name once my friend (and co-producer) Bob Charde goaded me into action. The film follows our previous successful collaboration, *Good Morning* (2007). Time spent developing a project is never time wasted, as demonstrated by *Owl and Rabbit's* second life.

idea I had that centered around the odd-couple pairing of an owl and a rabbit. For this pitch, Fred invited me to his office, where I showed him a proposal called *Owl and Rabbit Play Checkers.* With this project, I took Fred's advice to heart. It was all about character. There was only enough plot to set the characters into action, and then allow the characters to take center stage. I felt especially cheeky because the story depicted an ordinary day in their lives: a date to play checkers. My feeling was, If I can make that work, then I've got something.

You Did It!

At the conclusion of this pitch, in which I'd summarized the story in less than two minutes, Fred's eyebrows raised. "You did it! You did it!" he exclaimed. "This is terrific. I'm going to send it to Eric Homan in L.A. for him to check out." Fred runs his company out of an office in New York City, but the main production leg is in Los Angeles and is overseen by Frederator's vice president of development, Eric Homan. Many weeks went by, and I didn't hear any news from Mr. Homan. In the meantime, I scheduled another meeting with Fred, this time to show him a film I had just made with animator Dale Clowdis. Our film, *Scout Says*, was an outgrowth of a pitch project called *Hard to Swallow*, and detailed the misadventures of a trio of unlikely backyard animal friends: a bossy bird, a dim-witted cat, and a spineless (get it?) worm. Fred enjoyed the film and encouraged us to show it to Eric Homan after we mentioned that we would be in L.A. the following month, pitching some ideas to networks. Fred told me that while I was in L.A., I should be sure to ask Eric Homan about my *Owl and Rabbit* pitch. Fred runs his own company, but he was asking me to talk to someone else about the fate of a project for which he had professed love. I prepared myself for bad news.

Once in L.A., Dale and I were delighted to discover that Eric Homan was a swell guy. He spent two hours giving us a full tour of Nickelodeon studios (where Frederator is encamped) and also took the time to look at *Scout Says*. At the time, Frederator was not yet ready to embark on its next round of *Oh Yeah! Cartoons*. We were only hoping to plant a seed and to entice the Frederator execs to want to work with us when they were ready.

Eric then turned to my *Owl and Rabbit Play Checkers* pitch. "This is great. And a couple of months ago, we would have done this, but now we're looking for stuff that doesn't skew quite this young," he explained. I felt like Bart in *The Simpsons* when the Hollywood director says, "Congratulations, Bart Simpson: you're our new Fallout Boy! That's what I'd be saying to you if you weren't an inch too short. . . . Next!"

I was euphoric a few months earlier when Fred had seemed to love this pitch, and I had walked out of the meeting believing I'd made a sale. Positive feedback on a pitch can be intoxicating. It's hard not to let hubris settle in and induce us to build a case for how it can't possibly go anywhere but up. In my case the evidence was my reputation as a director on the number one preschool series, my history illustrating children's books, the brilliance of my project, the fact that Frederator needed to make dozens of books to fulfill its requirements to Nick Jr., and the fact that Fred seemed to love it. All this combined to make one powerfully convincing argument. However, as the old adage goes, expect nothing and you won't be disappointed. As creators, it's our responsibility to keep our expectations in check. Until a contract is offered and signed, we have no guarantees (and even then, it's iffy).

Shortly after my return to New York, Allworth Press greenlighted my proposal to write the first-ever comprehensive career guide for animation artists working in North America. I agreed to write the book within a year, splitting my time between freelancing, a full-time job directing animation on Jim Jinkins's series *Pinky Dinky Doo* at Cartoon Pizza, teaching commitments, and working on a personal film. With such a busy time ahead of me, developing and pitching new projects was the furthest thing from my mind.

I'm Dying to Do a Short with Dave Levy

Some months later I invited Fred to be a guest speaker at my SVA animation career class. He was a galvanizing presence, challenging everyone in the room to make choices. If they wanted to work on hits, he said, they had to move to L.A. and work in the center of the industry. In the next breath, he taunted me for staying in New York City despite all the advice he'd previously given me against it. Fred was only half-kidding. At one point Fred was challenged by a student who felt New York could become a full-blown rival for Hollywood production. "Then go do it," Fred said. "I believe you can do it if you set your mind to it." Ironically, a few months later, this student moved to Los Angeles.

Frederator was looking for thirty-nine new shorts, and Fred encouraged everyone in the class to pitch him. Then he said, "I'm dying to do a short with Dave Levy." As I started to turn red, Fred poked me in the shoulder and said, "Do you hear what I'm saying? I'm serious."

On the subway ride home I was electrified. I started browsing through the undeveloped ideas in my head, but nothing came. When I got home, I told the news to my wife, Debbie, and we developed a short centered on the idea of two weird kids at school who also happen to be rivals and next-door neighbors. We chose a couple of historical figures as the blueprints for our protagonists: Teddy Roosevelt and Annie Oakley. I whipped up some placeholder designs for *Teddy and Annie* and we beat out a story together over the next few days. Once we had a script in place, we hired storyboard artist Otis Brayboy to create a pitch board. One of the peculiarities of Frederator's pitch process is its insistence on looking at pitches in storyboard form only. Development executives aren't asking for a full-fledged production board drawn in a clean line with every shot carefully depicted. Instead, their ideal pitch board is a rough, simplified storyboard, maybe thirty three-panel pages long.

Show art for *Teddy and Annie*, which I co-created with Deborah M. Staab.

In the meantime, Eric Homan e-mailed, also expressing hope that I would pitch Frederator. When I called back, he told me, "As we planned what we wanted for these thirty-nine shorts, we kept coming back to your short, *Scout Says.*" My expectations went up another notch. Not only was Fred pulling for me, but, now, Eric was, too! Of course, I knew my partners and I would still have to deliver the goods, but I never doubted our abilities to do that.

Around the same time, I had lunch with my friend, writer Richard Gorey. I mentioned the *Teddy and Annie* pitch and Rich asked me if I planned to pitch anything else. There was an idea that I was kicking around called *Tad and His Dad,* about a family that runs into trouble when Tad misuses real magic and permanently changes his dad into a rabbit. Little Tad doesn't have the skills to change him back, and hilarity ensues. It was just a shell of a creation, but Rich was so enthusiastic about it that I asked him to come on board as a co-writer and co-creator. Again, once we had a final script, Otis Brayboy went to work on the storyboard. *Teddy and Annie* and *Tad and His Dad* were ready for pitching at almost the same time.

My enthusiasm for pitching to Frederator soon spread to others working at Cartoon Pizza on *Pinky Dinky Doo,* where storyboard supervisor Diane Kredensor already had a deal with Frederator for one of her Nick Jr. children's books. She had made it to the top three books chosen to compete for one series slot, which ultimately was won by Bob Boyle's *Wow! Wow! Wubsy!* Soon, she and her writing partner, Dana Galin (also her coauthor on the Nick Jr. book), had a pitch of their own, *Call Me Bessie!* It seemed very salable. A few months later, four other Cartoon Pizza employees pitched to Frederator, and we all cheered each other on. With thirty-nine cartoon slots to fill, there was enough love to go around.

You Didn't Want It Bad Enough

At the beginning of our pitch meeting for *Teddy and Annie*, Fred said to me: "How come you never came back when I gave you notes on your old pitches?"

"I was busy with work. I had full-time jobs as well as freelance, teaching, and . . ."

Fred cut me off, "No. You didn't want it bad enough. You would have come back to re-pitch if you wanted it bad enough."

In reality, it's kind of a reckless idea to prioritize pitching above all else. Additionally, a creator should not automatically bend to or address every criticism and suggestion she hears in a pitch meeting. Regardless, Fred soon dropped it and threw a few "getting to know you" questions toward my wife. After that I thanked Fred for the opportunity, and as I was about to open the pitch folder, Fred said, "This is my favorite part of the pitch. I have no idea what you have. You could have the next huge hit in there."

On that note, we pitched. I acted out the board and Debbie caught all the grounders that got by me. Fred applauded when the pitch was done, which I later learned is his habit. Then he gave us his list of notes: the character design looked a little young; he wanted more contrast between the characters and suggested giving them different goals; we should consider that distinct good guys and villains help a pitch find its focus. Our story pitted Teddy and Annie against each other, competing to win the school science fair. Each character had an enormous ego and would do anything to win; it was a private war between strong-willed characters. We assured Fred that there were more details in the full storyboard that might help to fill in the gaps. After the meeting, Debbie and I brainstormed on Fred's suggestions. We came up with a few new spins on the characters and hatched up new plots for them. Yet, we both assumed that *Tad and His Dad* would have a better shot because the titular characters were engaged in the simple sort of good-versus-bad scenario that Fred seemed to like.

My rough design of Seymour Spells, the host of the magical idol competition from *Tad and His Dad*.

Tad and His Dad

A week after Debbie and I pitched *Teddy and Annie*, Rich Gorey and I were ready to pitch *Tad and His Dad*. We had spent months passing script drafts back and forth and we were very proud of the results. Tad and his dad were a father and son magic act who enter a contest in hopes of becoming America's next magical idols. Nine-year-old Tad was born with the gift of "real" magic, but because using real magic would be cheating in a stage magic competition, Dad forbids Tad to use his special abilities in their act. Once a villainous pair of contestants shows up, sabotaging everyone's acts, Tad is hard-pressed to keep his promise. What's a magical boy to do?

After some banter, Rich took on the main pitching duties for *Tad and His Dad*. Although Rich hadn't presented a cartoon pitch before, he's an excellent public speaker with a lot of showmanship. Instead of reading our exact dialogue and description, he described character motivation and back-story, almost acting as a narrator. I jumped in a few times, but realized that Rich and I had made a mistake in not rehearsing better. We were having trouble striking the balance between laying it all out and being fresh and spontaneous.

Fred clapped when we finished and gave us his list of notes. "Okay, you've got some strong elements here. I love the name, Tad." Then Fred explained how we needed to better define the rules of the magic. He noted that his major contribution to *The Fairly OddParents* was in helping creator Butch Hartman work out the rules of the magic.

In response to Fred's other issues with the characters and plot, I tried to assure him that he would find what he was looking for in our full storyboard, of which I had brought two copies so Fred could read it or send it on to L.A. "Oh, no," Fred responded. "That's what you said last time, and it wasn't in the boards." Instead, Fred encouraged us to come back and re-pitch *Tad and His Dad*. At some point in the meeting, Fred looked at me, and perhaps responding to the look on my face, said, "I hope you didn't think that I would pick up whatever you brought in just because I said I wanted you to pitch to me." No, I hadn't thought that, but I did believe in the talents of my team, myself, and the projects we'd created.

Richard Gorey and I repeated our process of e-mailing draft after draft of revisions to each other until we were happy with the new script, which I used to prepare a new version of the storyboard to pitch. This time we decided that I would pitch the board to Fred.

Here's How Your Deal Will Work

Between our first and second pitch of *Tad and His Dad*, Diane Kredensor and Dana Galin pitched their idea, *Call Me Bessie!* From Diane's description it sounded like their meeting had gone very well. Fred didn't have any issues or concerns about their project. Instead, he sent it on to L.A. where Eric Homan and Larry Huber (co-executive producer of *Oh Yeah! Cartoons*) could weigh in. A week later, Diane found out that her short was greenlighted. It felt like a shared victory, and her success gave me renewed hope. I was pretty excited when Rich and I re-pitched *Tad and His Dad*, but in my wildest expectations, I couldn't have imagined what Fred said at the conclusion: "This is great. It's like night and day from the last time you brought this in. I still have a few concerns with it, but they don't worry me. Leave me a copy of this to send to L.A."

If the meeting had ended right there it would have been positive enough, but what followed was like a dream come true. Fred said, "Here's how your deal will work." For the next half-hour, Fred told us all the ins and outs of the deal they were offering us. First, he told us to get a lawyer and to figure out whether we wanted to be represented together or separately. Next, Fred stated that I would be more involved than Rich, because I would be the director working on the pilot for the duration of production. Rich would provide writer duties at various stages.

"You'll need to decide where you'll be doing this: New York or L.A.," Fred continued. Then he mentioned there was no negotiating because he was making thirty-nine different shorts. "If we allowed creators to negotiate, then we'd be making fewer shorts. Each deal is the same." That sounded reasonable and logical to Rich and me. Thirty minutes later, we shook hands with Fred and were on our way. At the elevator bank outside of Frederator's offices, Rich and I looked at each other in disbelief and shared a victory hug. We were following in Diane and Dana's footsteps with *Call Me Bessie!*

The Beginning of the End

A couple of weeks went by and Rich and I remained on cloud nine. Then, one day, Eric Homan sent an e-mail from L.A., reading: "So, Larry and I both took a look at your board and liked it pretty well. We're thinking we should have a phone call with you, Rich, and Fred toward the end of this week or the beginning of next week to go over the board in detail. It'd be great to have you guys on board. What do you think?" What did I think? I was a little confused. Judging from our conversation with Fred, weren't we already on board? I had a sinking feeling in my stomach.

Fred called me at my Cartoon Pizza office to explain. "Okay, here's the deal. We're making your picture. But Larry has some problems with it. Can you and Rich come down to my office this week so we can have a conference call with Eric and Larry?" Fred's reassurance that we were still in business went a long way for me.

Rich and I showed up in Fred's office that week for the conference call. Before we got the L.A. team on the phone, Fred told us that he was surprised by Larry's reaction. He gave us every indication that it was a small bump in the road. Eric and Larry joined us on the phone, and Larry explained that *Tad and His Dad* already had enough potential to carry a series, but he had a few story notes to go over. After the meeting, Rich confessed his love of our last draft, wondering aloud if we shouldn't stick up for our approach. I pushed us forward to complete a third draft storyboard based on the latest notes. My thinking was, the sooner we address their concerns, the sooner we'll get to make the short.

Over the next six months, Rich and I toiled through six more drafts of revisions. With new revisions came new notes. From L.A. we received notes like, "Can you change Tad and Dad's finale from juggling live chain saws to something less dangerous and more typical of a magic act?" We changed it to a water tank escape trick. Of course, as time wore on, some doubt naturally crept into our heads. Yet when I checked in with Fred, he reassured me, "After *Pinky Dinky Doo*, you're working for us."

Early on in our six months of revisions, I had a bold thought. One of my great musical heroes is former Lovin' Spoonful frontman John B. Sebastian. He wrote and performed some of my favorite songs: "Daydream," "Summer in the City," "Do You Believe in Magic," "Welcome Back," and scads of others. I took a shot and contacted Sebastian's management company and, to my delight, he was interested. We ended up having several meetings, phone conversations, and lunches that resulted in Sebastian writing a theme song for *Tad and His Dad* with the understanding that our deal with Frederator was forthcoming. As an added bonus, it turned out both Fred and Eric were fans of Sebastian's work.

Next, I set about figuring out where to produce our pilot. I was having a great experience working at Cartoon Pizza, so I approached its affable president, Jack Spillum, to see if it was possible to produce *Tad and His Dad* at the Cartoon Pizza studio. *Pinky Dinky Doo* was going to wrap its first season in a few months, so the timing seemed just right.

A week after Cartoon Pizza gave me a simple production contract to review, everything changed.

If I Was a Smoker, I Would Have Lit Up

With only a few weeks of employment left on *Pinky Dinky Doo* and six months of revisions on *Tad and His Dad* in the can, I asked Fred for an update on our project. The next day Fred called me back with Eric on the line. After over an hour of them explaining why they were not going to be making my picture, I was left with the renewed understanding that pitching is not something to depend on. Somewhere along the line I'd forgotten that.

"I asked Larry if we were ready to do your picture," Fred said. "He told me, 'Sure, I can make it work.' So, then I said, 'No, we won't make his picture, because if you have to fix it for Dave, then he's not ready.'

Creators need to be self-sufficient, Fred explained, and not dependent upon their partners' notes. Here, my willingness to tackle revisions in cooperation with the rotating ring of producers, each of his own mind on what the film should be, was evidence against my readiness as a creator.

Thinking of a story Fred had told me about two creators who went on to make shorts for him after initially being rejected over and over again, I had resolved to be accommodating and enthusiastic in addressing changes. Of the two creators from the story, one had become the creator of a hit series for Frederator. The other creator gave up after his third pitch, but when Fred called him on the phone, asking if he knew why Fred hadn't bought one of his shorts, the creator answered, "Because you think my work is more complicated than it really is and you don't realize how simple it will be in the execution."

"Right," replied Fred, before inviting the creator back to pitch again. When the creator showed up with another pitch, Fred put his hand over the envelope, before he could pull out the pitch, and said, "Stop. I bought it." And a deal was made, sight unseen.

In my overly apt mind, I had taken the lesson of these stories to be that all the hard work and determination won these creators their greenlights. If I had thought about it more clearly, I would have realized that these were also stories of power and personality. Because there are no rules on how shows are picked up in the world of development, a lot is left up to the personal discretion of the person who wields the power.

The bottom line is that it's one thing to "want it bad enough" and quite another thing to be a doormat. At that moment, I resented the whole Frederator team as well as myself. Now, I had to explain to Rich Gorey, friends, family, coworkers, Cartoon Pizza, and John Sebastian what had happened. I felt dizzy. I felt sick. I don't recall too much of my response to Fred and Eric on the phone. I know they could hear the emotion in my voice. I do remember saying, "Well, I know it's not possible to talk someone into picking up a project they don't want." Fred and Eric assured me that they still wanted to work with me and that I should pitch them again.

I stepped outside and bought a coffee. I suppose if I was a smoker, I would have lit up. I walked the block a few times, not wanting to return to

Post-Frederator, Otis Brayboy drew this storyboard page for my revamped *ManGoofs* pitch to Cartoon Network's Cartoonstitute shorts program.

my job right away. I was furious with Frederator, disappointed in myself, and very determined to succeed with or without them.

Of Men and ManGoofs

You might think me odd, or a glutton for punishment, but I was inspired to pitch Frederator again. In my estimation, Fred and his team were wrong to reject our cartoon, yet in no way was my confidence shattered. I was grateful to Frederator for reawakening my desire to create and develop pitches. Before they came along, I had had no serious plans to pitch anything.

Climbing back in the development saddle, I thought of Dale Clowdis and our film *Scout Says*. It was the very film that Eric Homan claimed as an influence in their quest for thirty-nine new shorts. Since I had been the main writer of *Scout Says*, it was time for Dale to try his hand at writing. He drafted a nice script based on an old premise for the pitch. We would continue with the characters of *Scout Says*: Scout the bird, Smudge the cat, and Osmond the worm, engaged in an unnatural and uneasy friendship.

In our new script, Osmond's apple, which he uses as a pseudo-body, is destroyed, so Smudge promptly fits Osmond into a new apple. But there's already a worm in it—a treacherous hipster named Larry, who is immediately popular with Scout and Smudge and sets out to estrange Osmond from his friends. At the pitch meeting, Fred ripped the pitch apart, encouraging us come back with changes. Dale and I decided to let this pitch die.

Still determined to nab a Frederator short and prove that I did "want it bad enough," I asked Dale's permission to revisit an old creation of ours, *Mangoose*. It had been our very first pitch together in 2000. The Mangooses were a pair of other-dimensional brothers who snuck into our world to escape their Mama's oppressive rule back home. Much like David Banner in TV's *The Incredible Hulk*, the Mangoose brothers move from town to town, trying to fit in, and always making a mess of it all. They want nothing more than to assimilate, blend in, and grab their share of the American dream, but as wacky other-dimensional beings, they can't get anything right.

Perhaps my favorite thing about *Mangoose* was our designs. The characters had an impish quality to them and we tried to give them a crazy-behind-the-eyes, Marx Brothers look. Both Fred and Eric often cite Bugs Bunny as a classic example of a successful character vehicle. Trying to conceive a project as simple and effective as that, I created a new vehicle for *Mangoose* and renamed the project *ManGoofs*. This time, Eric and Fred allowed me to submit pitches in the simpler, faster script form, and I e-mailed the *ManGoofs* script their way, along with some sample artwork. Weeks later, Eric wrote back, "Some funny gags. But it looks like you're trying too hard." As Freddie Mercury sang, another one bites the dust.

Meanwhile, several pitches made by Cartoon Pizza employees were also failing to set Frederator on fire. Even Diane Kredensor and Dana Galin found difficulty repeating the success of *Call Me Bessie!* Diane later realized that a couple of their attempts were not born of inspiration, but simply an attempt to score another pilot. Their final try, however, had loads of potential. In fact, I had lunch with a recent Frederator intern who discovered their pitch in a folder while cleaning up the office. He read it and thought it was amazing. "I can't believe they didn't make this," he exclaimed. A few other Frederator creators were more fortunate and went on to create more than one short for the series. All of these creators happened to live in Los Angeles and therefore had access to Eric Homan and Larry Huber on a daily basis. In New York, we creators wondered how important a role geography was playing in the matter.

I Feel Terrible

At this time, my wife and I had the good fortune of discovering producer Val Lewton's classic RKO thrillers made in the 1940s. These beautifully shot black-and-white films were stylish, adult, and very dark. Lewton's work started to invade our subconscious, ultimately leading us to create a new character for yet another series pitch.

I created designs while Debbie, Rich Gorey, and I collaborated on the script. Cartoon Network's *Codename: Kids Next Door* storyboard artist Matt Peters created the board and we were soon ready to make our final pitch to Frederator. With only six spots left from the original bonanza of thirty-nine, time was running out.

Each time I pitch, I try to do something a little different than the time before. This time, I brought in the talented writer, performer, comedienne, and voice-over actress Becky Poole, who agreed to act out the pitch for Fred. Over the next few days, Becky and I snuck in rehearsal time so we could prepare for the meeting.

Despite my track record at Frederator, I believed that I was learning a lot with each pitch attempt. This final pitch felt like the culmination of an entire experience. After Becky and I acted out the pitch, Fred clapped and then listed the many problems he saw in the short. As someone who rarely loses his temper, I have to admit that this repeat of Fred's dos and don'ts finally pushed me to snap at him.

"You have a very limited view of what a cartoon is!" I yelled. "Just because you think there's only one way to make a successful cartoon doesn't make it so! Your narrow view is why you'll say NO to this!"

In the couple of years I'd known Fred, this was the first time I'd seen him go speechless. All the frustrations and disappointments that I had suppressed by pushing forward came crashing down on me.

Becky had to get back to work, and wisely beat her retreat.

Even under the best of circumstances, success in the world of development is not a sure thing. You also have to adjust your expectations accordingly, which is what I learned as I left the meeting exhausted, emotional, and defeated.

Fred said he'd send the pitch along to Los Angeles. I had very little hope that Eric or Larry would feel any differently about the pitch, so I was not surprised when Eric e-mailed his notes, concluding with, "You won't have time to revise this because we are now out of shorts," and, "I feel terrible." I wrote Eric back telling him not to worry, because the opportunity was mine to lose.

What's It All About, Alfie?

The rejection of a project is no excuse to burn bridges or become enemies with the development executive and his network. Shortly after Frederator passed on *Tad and His Dad*, Fred rang me up to schedule a lunch where he treated me to a nice meal at a fine restaurant. Months after my final pitch was rejected, I took Eric to breakfast while he was in New York on business. It was nice to connect with both of them outside of a pitch. A year later, I moderated an animation career panel for ACM SIGGRAPH (Association for Computing Machinery's Special Interest Group on Graphics and Interactive Techniques), at which Fred was my invited guest. That same month, I hosted an ASIFA-East event celebrating Frederator's thirty-nine new shorts. We packed the audience with 200 people, all eager to hear about the development process and see films, and to meet creators such as Manny Galan, Alan Goodman, Bill Plympton, Dan Meth, Diane Kredensor, and Dana Galin. At one point in the evening, I asked Bill Plympton if Frederator gave him any notes during the pitch process. "They worried it was 'too young.' I said, 'No, it isn't.' That was the last note they gave," Bill answered.

Interestingly enough, the creator making the biggest splash was not in attendance. His name was Pendleton ("Pen") Ward and his Frederator short, *Adventure Time*, was the toast of the festival circuit and a viral phenomenon on YouTube, where fans have continued to post it despite MTV Networks's efforts to keep taking the short down. Fred told the story of Pen's pitch. "I didn't want to do his short. I didn't get it. I told Pen what he'd have to change, and he said, 'No.' Then Eric cornered me in his office and said, 'We have to do this.' I still didn't get it, but I trusted Eric. We made the short and it turns out I was wrong."

This is a good window into the greenlight process because it shows different experiences from creator to creator and project to project. Like the stories earlier in this chapter, personal taste and the power that wields it played a big part in *Adventure Time*'s success. All creators are dependent

The title art from Pen Ward's wonderfully whimsical Frederator short, *Adventure Time*. Ward demonstrated a strong vision both in the pitch meeting and in the execution of his film. Copyright 2008, Viacom International, Inc. All rights reserved.

upon an executive acting as a cheerleader on their behalf, as Eric did with Pen's story. Fred told another story that night. "Our generous host is being very kind, but the truth is that sometimes we make mistakes, and in his case, we should have just made his first pitch into a film. All we did was mess it up."

If I hadn't been so accommodating to their notes, maybe Frederator would have made *Tad and His Dad* into a short or maybe that would have scuttled the deal even sooner. Only one thing is certain: I've learned the importance of adhering to a strong vision while at the same being open to feedback. One should not automatically address nor battle every note. A creator should use his singular point of view as a compass to guide him through all notes, big and small. My blind willingness to address six months of revisions on *Tad and His Dad* proved I didn't fully trust my talents and those of my collaborators. If I couldn't do that, how could I expect Frederator to get on board with my project? My meltdown occurred when I gave away my power to Fred, Eric, and Larry. How could I not have been let down? How could I expect Fred and his company to be in the Dave Levy business more sincerely than Dave Levy? The most difficult part of being a creator is not always creating a project and readying it for pitching. It might be far more challenging to manage our expectations through the development process, navigating all the highs and lows that will inevitably come our way. I'm prepared to do that because I'm sincerely in the Dave Levy business. But you don't have to be; insert your name in place of mine.

Judging from Fred's words at the ASIFA-East event, I may not have been the only one who learned a lesson from all this. Fred and Eric have each expressed regret at how things turned out, and at the end of the day, maybe we all learned that we were not the right fit for each other at that point in time. Not only do I respect and admire them, I still hope we can collaborate on a project in the future.

Alan Goodman, someone who did get to make a short for Frederator that year, offers this advice that makes a fine last word for this chapter: "The thing you have to remember is, if the buyer doesn't like it, that doesn't mean anything at all. It just wasn't a match that day, that's all. If you are good, and you believe in your work, get another meeting with someone else. Go see that buyer with another project, but don't take it personally. The successful creators never do."

Chapter 8

The Option or Paper Development Deal

"The development process is very important for us. It lets us get in on the ground floor to work on something and really see if there's a spark there. That's where we can take a risk. There's less opportunity for risk once a project is in production."

—**Athena Georgaklis, manager of original production, Teletoon Canada, Inc.**

As is often the case in the world of development, there is no single answer to the question of what you can expect from a first-phase greenlight. If you are Tom Warburton, creator of Cartoon Network's *Codename: Kids Next Door*, you might get a pilot deal or even a series deal right after pitching. Creators such as Warburton have earned that right. Linda Simensky, vice president of children's programming at PBS, elaborates, "If a series is pitched by someone we are already working with, we may determine we are comfortable with that producer and move ahead to a series without a pilot. But when we have questions about a show or a creator, we might ask for a pilot or some further development to answer those questions."

For the rest of us, it's a little (or a lot) different. The most typical first phase of a greenlight would normally be an option for paper development. Paper development refers to creating further designs, storyboards, scripts, revisions to the pitch bible, etc. In short, creating all the materials

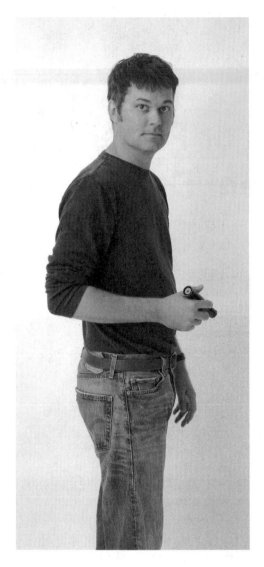

Mo Willems, about to draw up some trouble. Today, he's best known for his Caldecott Honor–winning picture books, *Don't Let the Pigeon Drive the Bus!* and *Knuffle Bunny: A Cautionary Tale*, but he's also the winner of six Emmy awards for his writing on *Sesame Street* and his roles as the creator of Cartoon Network's *Sheep in the Big City* and former head writer of *Codename: Kids Next Door*. "Mo" stuff is on the way. Photo by Marty Umans.

without actually producing a pilot. Until recently, the knowledge that options for paper development existed drove me crazy. If networks did extensive redevelopment on an idea once it was optioned (which is often the case), that must mean that pitches lucky enough to secure an option are not necessarily perfect. For a long time, I felt that this reality entitled me to an option.

As the years passed and I accumulated more practical experience in the industry, my pitches gradually improved and executives started to respond very positively in the pitch meetings. If their enthusiasm in the meeting alone could create a deal, I'd have five shows on the air already. I'm in good company, because even a world-class talent such as Mo Willems has experienced the same situation. Willems shares, "Recently, I ran into an executive who I'd pitched to a few years ago. She told me that my pitch (which was made solely with plastic spoons) was the best, most innovative she'd ever experienced. Fine—I feel all warm and fuzzy, but it's not like she bought the show."

The reality is that not all pitches, however warmly received, will be granted an option. The network and network executives need to be convinced to option a project. On the surface, optioning a project seems like a smallish commitment. The monies paid to the creator are relatively small and the work is spread out over periods as long as a year. However, my network option paid a fair price, and if you add to that the network's legal expenses, it starts to make sense why more projects are not optioned. The option represents a sincere desire by the network executives to further explore your idea at their own cost or risk. Now, I see the option as a gift to your project, because the network is paying you to do further development on your idea.

Rules Sometimes Rule

Most any animator can spend a few hours and bust out an independently made cartoon. Okay, maybe it is only a few seconds long, but it is a film nonetheless and could be posted on YouTube or a personal Web site. In this exercise in total creative freedom, there's no pitching, development deal, waiting for contracts, or the need to negotiate through network or client notes. In short, making a film on your own has very little in common with how the creative process works once you sign a contract with a network or entertainment company.

To sign a development deal is to take on the obligations of that partnership. The first thing to know is that you'll be giving up your autonomy when it comes to creative freedom. It's very rare that creators are hired to pump out a show with nary a creative note coming from the network. The network holds the purse and has the means of distribution and promotion. It might seem like an independent animator making films in his bedroom and posting them online would be immune to working in this traditional development model, yet despite even millions of online views of your work, the Internet is not a means to an end when it comes to success. A far more likely scenario is that your successful Internet property will be optioned for development by a traditional cable or broadcast network. All at once, a project born of creative freedom will enter the world of development notes and all manner of creative input and interference.

Before we go any further, there is one more myth to bust here: that network notes are bad. Network creative notes may be good or bad, just like we may have good or bad ideas ourselves. Do not fall prey to outdated "us versus them" scenarios that make heroes out of the artists and villains out of the network suits. An example I like to point out of creative notes being a positive thing is the original Nickelodeon's *The Ren & Stimpy Show*, created by John Kricfalusi. Tension between the network and the creator of this legendary series over the boundaries of appropriateness and good taste resulted in a masterful season of episodes. Because *The Ren & Stimpy Show* was on Nickelodeon, it was a children's show. Kricfalusi's sensibility was more irreverently adult. Nickelodeon's notes and rules helped shape the creative process because they gave its creator boundaries in which to create and to push up against. The resulting mixture brought out the best in Kricfalusi and his creative team and the result was a groundbreaking series, which still casts a shadow of influence to this day.

It was interesting when *The Ren & Stimpy Show* was briefly revived on Spike TV in a new incarnation called *Ren & Stimpy "Adult Party Cartoon"* and the project proved to be a ratings disappointment. Part of the problem was that Spike TV gave the series near total freedom to explore its "adult side." While there were always adult touches in the original series, it never wallowed in them. The new version was all but consumed by excess and was a failure with the network and the intended audience. To be fair, another factor in the failure may have been Spike TV's fleeting commitment to animation. The struggling network abandoned its entire animated programming block one year out of the gate.

Managing Creative Notes

Anytime you hear someone tell stories of "stupid network executives" giving bad notes and ruining a show, remember that the network's partner was the creator. The creator has an obligation to the show's success, too. In addition to the creative work of writing and conceiving a show, the process by which creators collaborate with their network development

Early pitch art for my creation *Fiona Finds Out,* which I revised over the course of many months as I readied the project for its eventual pick-up.

executives can be an art form in and of itself. Being an outsider to development success for ten years, I had a good theory based on lots of observation: the development process doesn't stop once you sign a deal. If you've pitched at all, you've probably been given friendly notes and advice on your projects by development executives. After signing a deal, it's pretty much the same situation, only with the benefit of both parties having been bound into sincerity by a business relationship.

To score my first development deal, I prepared a mini pitch bible containing six pieces of show art; descriptions of the characters, world, and rules; episode synopses; and one complete pilot script. This pitch, a proposal for a preschool series, was the result of nine months of self-development. For creators, it's tempting to think that we've got it all mapped out, but the best pitch elements are only an appetizer to try to interest a buyer in your series. It behooves us to think of our pitches as being a draft—not *the* draft.

Once the network representatives and I had signed a short-form version of the contract, a meeting was scheduled between their development executive and me. This was the development executive who had shepherded my project up the chain of command. Aside from me, there was probably no one who knew the pitch better. Our first meeting was about an hour and was mainly to map out an attack plan. The network had entered into an agreement with me to develop my idea toward producing five four-minute short films, which could be aired as interstitials. This was terribly exciting for me because as interstitials the films would be broadcast, filling in programming holes on the network lineup. It meant that my work would be seen on TV! So many development deals result in the production of test pilots made for boardrooms and focus groups only. The definitive description of five four-minute shorts gave us focus. We knew how many and how long.

My development executive suggested I begin by creating five premises for the shorts. In the original pitch elements, there were six synopses or premises already, with one scripted to full length. A funny thing happens to pitch bibles post-deal: they date very, very quickly. Of all the premises in the pitch bible, only one survived. The rest only served to help us determine areas we didn't wish to pursue. In a matter of weeks, we had our new premise list solidified. The next challenge was to take one premise and plug it into an outline for a four-minute short.

Don't React to Every Little Thing You Hear

This could be one of the single most important pieces of advice in this book: not everything you hear in a conversation is something you have to respond to, agree with, or challenge. Have you ever heard the expression "thinking out loud"? Well, that's often what happens on both sides of the table in the development process. Ideas, suggestions, and criticisms are offered that don't always need to be answered. Some of them just belong homeless, hanging in the air. Wave to them as they drift by, but don't feel the need to honor every word with a response. You need to trust that the good ideas will bubble to the top and won't go unnoticed.

Sounds reasonably possible, right? Well, add one more factor that makes things even more challenging: attitude. How was something said? What was the emotional context? One creator's story illustrates the potential pitfalls. The creator (who we won't name) met with a development executive to go over her first script. It was a first draft, so there was a lot to iron out and discuss. The executive was open and frank in identifying the areas that weren't working yet. When it came to giving redirection, the executive was vague, offering up an array of multiple (and often conflicting) possibilities. This can be a great scenario because we can read it as the executive not forcing a specific solution on us. It allows the creator to gather her thoughts and pull a solution from her own vision, which is what "creator-driven" is supposed to mean. However, things became more challenging for the creator in this story. When the executive wondered aloud in an exasperated manner, "Will we ever get there?," it was a worrisome thing for the creator to hear.

Did those words imply doubt that the creator could pull it off or an indication that the executive was cooling to the project? These were natural questions for any creator to ask in that circumstance, but not questions that need to be asked out loud. The creator's job is to sift through all the unimportant talk and get to the real message—in this case, what wasn't working in the rough script. The rest can be chalked up to personality. A shopper waiting in a long line at the supermarket may ask, "Will this line ever move?" But he probably knows it will move and is moving. Our mission as creators is twofold: to preserve and value the relationship with the executive and the network, and to serve the project above all else. When the project wins, both sides of the table win.

There are times when a phrase like, "Will we ever get there?" can indicate a waning enthusiasm for a project or a growing lack of faith in its creator. But so what? The onus is still on us to make our best effort and demonstrate the surety of our voice and vision as creators. Be open to collaboration, but trust the instincts that got you this far in the first place.

I Dreamed I Swallowed a Pillow and When I Woke Up, My Deal Was Gone

Well, okay, there was no dream the night before, but it is true that my deal vaporized into thin air overnight. What happened? The world of development, that's what happened. Slowly and steadily over the course of a year, I passed one development checkpoint after another, although not always on the first try. I was assigned five premises to write and got those approved in less than two months. Then we moved forward, turning our attention to a first test script. A couple of months later, we reached an approved script by the fourth draft. It was at this point that I was given the go-ahead to write the remaining four scripts, using the approved one as a model. Good news kept coming. My development executive arranged a breakfast date for us with an important network honcho from Los Angeles and asked me to "start thinking about where I wanted to produce the shorts." Pretty awesome, huh?

Around this time I had lunch with my pal Dale Clowdis, a good friend and past pitch partner. I filled him in on my success with this development deal and he was so excited for me. "We never got this far before!" he cheered, sharing in my happiness. It's a good way to look at it. I'd been developing shows for ten years and this deal was the first real breakthrough after a long journey through smoke and mirrors, with raised spirits always followed by dashed hopes. If I had been more sensible, I would have realized that if it ended here, as development so often does, that it would still be a major accomplishment, something to consolidate into a bigger success in the future. Instead, I set the bar a little higher in my mind. My goal was to make at least one of the five shorts.

Part of me saw the problem coming. Although I passed each development stage, there was always some struggle. My development executive often worried we had too much curriculum and not enough fun in the scripts. Each round we tweaked the script to better balance the two needs. On our last phone conversation she gave me a big script note. She wanted a major rewrite, further rebalancing to pump up the fun quotient yet again. I cooked up something I was happy with and sent it along to her and then waited. Just before a holiday, she e-mailed me that she still had problems with the concept and format of the show. Her remedy? Sending the pitch to her counterparts in Los Angeles for them to weigh in. Part of me worried this was the prelude to "goodbye," and that turned out to be the case when we spoke on the phone a few days later.

She was very sweet and supportive, affirming hers and the network's desire to work with me on a project. They had decided not to go forward with my shorts because of problems with the concept and because they didn't want to do a science-based preschool show. Then she started exploring ways we could work together or things I might want to pitch, suggesting we meet up right after the holiday to discuss it further. I appreciated all this very much and told her so. Unlike with the similar call from Frederator two years earlier (see chapter 7: Emotional Rescue), I felt able to have the discussion without reacting emotionally. Instead, I offered her a new plan.

"I totally understand the feedback, and I know there's a wide room for interpretation in such a subjective world as development. I don't fault the conclusions you came to at all, but I do have good reason why I'd like to try again."

"I'm listening," she said.

"Obviously, I believe in the project, but I also believe we didn't really explore all the possibilities. All our revisions worked within the same three-layer curriculum and format structure. Yes, we tried to boost the fun and find the right balance between fun and curriculum, but we only explored one way to do this. Also, the premises we narrowed down further pushed us towards a science-based show, but this was never how I felt about it. I never thought we were doing a science show. I think there's a lot left to explore here. Now, I don't know your network's development world as well as you. So, what I'm asking is: Is it futile for me to try some redevelopment scenarios on this project and show them to you? Is the door open for that?"

"Yes, I'd love to see what you'd like to try with this," she replied. "We'd be open to that."

"Great. Then what I'd like to do is explore some new directions."

"Why don't you give me that in outline form?" she suggested.

And it was just that simple: we had a plan. I also made sure to thank her for all her support, saying, "I have no expectations as to the outcome. But your faith in this project has meant a lot to me and I feel I owe it to both of us to give this another try."

I had mixed emotions after the phone call. There was a pitiful side to my position. I felt a bit like George Costanza's girlfriend in *Seinfeld*, when he tries to break up with her and she tells him, "No. We're not breaking up." Pitiful or not, I believed in myself and in my ability to solve this creative problem. There are no guarantees at any stage of the pitching and development process, so this wasn't such a new scenario in which to operate. As to whether or not it was a futile effort to try to revive this pitch at the network, it's never a waste of time to develop something for yourself. After all, the network's option on my idea would expire in a few short months. Whatever work I chose to continue doing would serve me in selling this project elsewhere.

It should not come as a shock to you that despite my efforts, this project was not revived at the network. Another creator who worked with this network believed I had been the victim of a power play between Los Angeles and New York development executives. Perhaps this was so. Many months later, I pitched this same project to a rival network, which

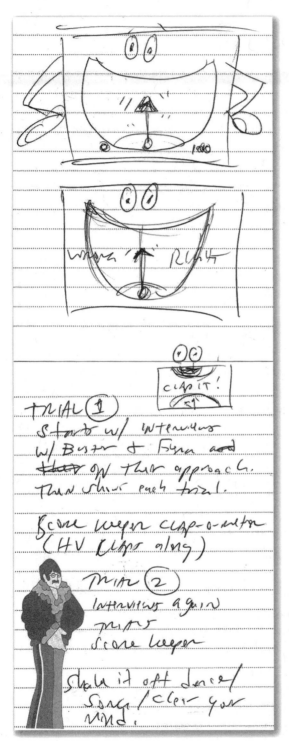

Now that the rights to *Fiona Finds Out* have reverted back to me, I am free to re-pitch the project elsewhere. Here are some new development notes I jotted down after a fun meeting with Linda Simensky at PBS Kids. Notice how I never leave home without my trusty Beatles notebook.

responded favorably. The new network development executive gave me some constructive feedback in hopes that I would return to re-pitch the property. As a lark, I decided to mention the last-ditch redevelopment plans I had created to try to save my original deal. The new development executive's eyes widened upon hearing them and exclaimed, "That's just the direction you ought to try." It was a good reminder that no work is ever wasted. I might just get my show on the air yet.

The Lifeline of Work

In my last book, *Your Career in Animation: How to Survive and Thrive*, I described how working on personal projects and freelance can help you manage creative feedback on a full-time job, the reason being that having other outlets for your creativity and other means of income allows you to put your main job in proper perspective. There is far less pain from taking criticism at work when your own creativity is not married to it. The

Assy McGee's self-portrait reveals his romantic side. Who says a show about an ass can't be well-rounded? *Assy McGee*, its logo, and all related characters and elements are trademarks of and © 2008 The Cartoon Network.

same is true when it comes to navigating the process of your development deal. As is often said in this book, development is slow and sometimes frustrating.

As my development deal fizzled out, I renewed my appreciation for work. During the many of months writing and rewriting scripts, waiting for feedback, and waiting for payment, my job was my rock. In fact, I barely noticed how much time was flying by. I would turn in a new script draft and then get happily pulled into a full-time job directing on a TV series. It was a fun dual existence; my own preschool show was in development while I was directing an Adult Swim series called *Assy McGee*. Each role allowed me to work different creative muscles and to wear different hats. Best of all, the full-time job paid me a weekly salary, something that development is not set up to do. As the writing notes trickled down on my development deal, my dual career allowed me to process those notes for what they were and to set about addressing them without putting all my creativity on the line.

I may not always have a choice, but I can't imagine engaging in pitching and development without having a full-time job to balance it. Pitching and development is speculation, and depending on it to pay your rent is reckless to say the least.

Nice Guys Don't Finish Last

A one-time successful TV series creator recently remarked in an interview that his one regret was not being a "gentleman creator." In other words, he regretted his handling of relationships, particularly with the network development executives. For a time, he was protected and enabled by a sympathetic network executive who also happened to be his friend. Once this support system had moved on, the creator was left stranded without an ally, and the worst aspects of his behavior went unfiltered. The creator was often arrogant and sometimes irrational, and he began to burn important bridges with individual development executives. This creator's potential for a continuous path of success was interrupted, perhaps permanently. As his relationships with the networks suffered, his deals suffered, and a pair of pilots became frozen in development limbo.

What does this tell us? (1) that relationships matter, and (2) that for the long haul, they matter just as much as the creator's other most important asset—her creative voice or vision. The creator's story above is not an isolated incident. In fact, there are worse stories of creators even being kicked off of their own successful series amid production. These are not stories of network greed, nor are they an unjust attempt to wrest away creative control. Difficult, erratic, and unreasonable creators close the chapters on their own careers and become cautionary tales.

Nobody is suggesting that one wins points strictly for being a nice guy or, at worst, a pushover. Creator Craig McCracken points out that the strongest shows always have a strong creator running things and, ultimately, this is what the network executives are looking for. McCracken cautions, "But, and this is a big but, don't forget it's their money they're spending on you. So, being a team player does an artist good."

Chapter 9

The Pilot

"One of the things I beat into myself was that while I was there in L.A., my purpose was to make these pilots. I was the first one into the studio, and the last to leave every day . . . mainly because if the pilots failed, I didn't want to say, 'Gee, I wish I had worked harder on those things.'"

—Tom Warburton, creator of *Codename: Kids Next Door*, Cartoon Network

Pilots are where the funny character described in the pitch bible must actually prove to be funny. In contrast, the reader of a pitch bible (most likely a development executive) uses his own imagination to picture how a cartoon might look, move, and sound. Because a pilot is a film, it allows its creator to set the pace, tone, and sequence by which all information is communicated and revealed. The burden of an animation pilot is that it must introduce the key characters and their conflicts, set up the world and its rules, and entertain its audience within two to eleven minutes. Brevity is not only a creative challenge—it is also an asset, because a pilot should show just enough to leave its audience begging for more.

Whether a pilot is produced for broadcast or for the exclusive eyes of executives or focus groups, it remains foremost a test film. The test is twofold: it is the network's test of the creator and also the creator's test of her ability to execute her vision. Often, we hear that it's not the strength of the idea that matters, but how well it's executed. Pitch bibles are meant

tHose Kids Next Door

KENNY and the CHIMP

Little is known about this group of five kids that operates out of the house next door to Kenny. This in itself is strange as no one knows which one lives there (if any) and no one has ever seen any trace of parent supervision. Depending on the item they have gotten their hands on that day they have called themselves The Catapult Kids, The Deep Fryer Five, The Chocolate Pudding Platoon, The Makeover Mafia, The Bucket of Brown Betty Bunch (don't ask) and many other monickers. No one name has stuck for very long. More likely just mischievous kids (with access to high end technology) then criminals (but don't be so sure) they are very secretive of their actions and are not friendly to outsiders, especially Kenny. On the other hand, Chimpy is always welcome amongst their ranks and the combination of his unintentional mischief with their deliberate shenanigans can cause a mess of unusual size. Fortunately, the kids can be somewhat easily outwitted and sent scrambling to regroup only to surface later with new deviltry and an even newer name.

PUDDING CANNON
PROPERTY OF U.S. MILITARY

A page of Tom Warburton's pitch for his first Cartoon Network pilot, *Kenny and the Chimp*, debuts a pack of side characters that would later become his hit series *Codename: Kids Next Door*. *Codename: Kids Next Door*, its logo, and all related characters and elements are trademarks of and © 2008 The Cartoon Network.

to show that the creator has the ability to execute her vision through words and still pictures. Based on that pitch bible (and all the other ducks needed to line up in a row), a development deal is offered, which (with a little luck) may lead to a pilot.

Bob and Margaret co-creator David Fine notes an interesting difference between pilot and series production: "Surprisingly, it was actually easier to write half-hour episodes than the pilot because the pilot was so precious that writing it was much more exacting. The series was also exacting, but because each episode was one story rather than *the* story, we felt more relaxed and could try different things." Similarly, *Blue's Clues* co-creator Traci Paige Johnson describes pilots as having to be perfect, adding, "It sometimes stifles your creativity because you're worried about taking too big of risks or trying something too different."

No Way to Make a Living

> "During the production of the pilot, I had four different production jobs. I didn't pocket a penny from the pilot. It all went directly to our lawyers!"
>
> —Amy Steinberg, co-creator of *Chickie Poo and Fluff: Barnyard Detectives* (Noggin)

Development deals do not pay a lot of money. This also is usually the case when it comes to producing pilots. There is no set rate for pilot production. The budgets vary throughout the industry depending on a variety of factors, including the creator's status (Seth MacFarlane will earn a lot more than a newcomer), intended audience (preschool or adult animation for ages eighteen to thirty-four often have the lowest TV budgets), whether it is for Web or TV broadcast. (Web budgets are routinely the lowest budgets—period.)

Shorts programs such as Frederator's *Random! Cartoons*, Cartoon Network's *Cartoonstitute*, and Disney TV's *Shorty McShorts' Shorts!* churn out pilots in large quantities—up to thirty-nine at a time. Even in such mass development, there is no set scale for pilot budgets. One shorts development program told me that all their budgets are equal, but then contradicted this by saying some creators had successfully negotiated better deals. Not a big shock to learn, but it did say something about the level

A still from Janet Perlman's Cartoon Network pilot, *Penguins Behind Bars*.
Penguins Behind Bars, its logo, and all related characters and elements are
trademarks of and © 2008 The Cartoon Network.

of honesty at this particular shorts program. That said, not all creators are
created equal, so it would be wrong to assume that everyone might have
the clout to negotiate a higher pay rate. Each of us comes from a different
vantage point, which is why it's a good idea to have a lawyer go over any
pilot deal to make sure it's as fair as possible.

One thing is certain—making a pilot often doesn't pay a living wage.
Diane Kredensor, co-creator of *Call Me Bessie!* for Frederator's *Random!
Cartoons* reports, "It afforded me a living wage for about three months,
but for the next six months I definitely picked up freelance to supplement
my income." Adam Peltzman created a pilot for Nick Jr., where his deal
included a writing fee and a producing fee. Peltzman says, "The project
was stretched out over a pretty long period of time, and ultimately those
fees don't amount to much on a weekly basis." During the production of
his pilot, Peltzman supplemented his income by continuing in his full-
time job as the head writer of Nick Jr.'s successful *Backyardigans* series. In
contrast, Janet Perlman, creator of the Cartoon Network pilot *Penguins
Behind Bars*, had a living wage built into her pilot production budget. "I

was devoted full-time to it. If I was working on other things, the production would have suffered," she explains, reminding this author that when it comes to animation pitching and development, there are no absolute truths.

Another creator used a split focus to her advantage. As a precaution at the start of production of *Private Eye Princess*, her second pilot for Cartoon Network, Debra Solomon delayed her own salary to prevent her pilot from running out of cash. She explains, "I was working as the supervising director on *Lizzie McGuire* while working on *Private Eye Princess*. In the end, the very generous deal I got from Cartoon Network made it possible for me to be paid a living wage retroactively after we delivered the show."

One creator I interviewed said that she and her independent animation studio plunked down their own significant funds to augment her pilot's meager budget. Why did they take this risk? They were the first pilot greenlighted in a new network's first commitment to building an animation block. At the time of their pilot's greenlight, they were told that the idea was completely in tune with the development mandate and that they would go forward to series. A week before this pilot's completion, at considerable extra cost and debt to the creator, the network informed her that they'd already killed her pilot. It wouldn't be broadcast. It wouldn't go to series.

This creator's experience is not an isolated incident. Creators often misperceive executives' promises as set in stone. This doesn't suggest that executives deliberately mislead creators, but a promise isn't a written contract. Some development executives are so used to being encouraging that they may make pledges they won't or can't keep. One executive said I had a greenlight on a pitch, and another told me that my development deal was moving forward to the pilot stage. Both turned out to be untrue. Until you have the contract stating the terms as fact, you have to manage your own expectations and curb your own enthusiasm so as not to fall prey to these traps. Unfortunately, this is a lesson most of us have to learn the hard way.

The Creator's Roles on a Pilot

"Our first pilot, *Utica Cartoon*, was made out of a little farmhouse in Rhode Island. The biggest challenge was in

It's not a turducken. It's a still from Fran and Will Krause's Cartoon Network pilot, *Utica Cartoon*, which was animated by a crew of animation cowboys including Jesse Schmal and Mike Overbeck. *Utica Cartoon*, its logo, and all related characters and elements are trademarks of and © 2008 The Cartoon Network.

running a production and being twenty-three years old. Our producer quit a few weeks into the production, so I ended up learning to be a producer."

—Fran Krause, co-creator of *Utica Cartoon* and *The Upstate Four* (Cartoon Network)

For some creators, a pilot might be their first film. TV- or Web-based episodic animation directors, and some independent filmmakers, are naturally most ready to helm a pilot because of their ample production experience with storytelling, composition, pacing, and timing. *Codename: Kids Next Door* creator Tom Warburton was a first-time creator when he made *Kenny and the Chimp*, his first pilot for Cartoon Network. But he had already directed, animated, and designed on scores of animated projects and series while working for J.J. Sedelmaier Productions, Buzzco Associates, and Jumbo Pictures. Work on Mike Judge's *Beavis & Butt-Head* and Jim Jinkins's *Doug*, as well as character designs on Sue Rose's *Pepper Ann*, are also among his credits.

It would be a risky time for any newcomer to try out running a production on her first pilot. A creator with a background exclusively in storyboards, art direction, design, or writing should stick to that area of expertise in embarking on a pilot. This doesn't mean that a creator shouldn't shadow every other part of a pilot's production. It's only natural that a creator would be interested in following all stages of production, not only for increased understanding but also to offer valuable input that only a creator can provide.

When co-creators Diane Kredensor and Dana Galin were offered a pilot for their creation *Call Me Bessie!*, it blasted the pair into uncharted waters. Galin served as the co-writer and co-producer but had no prior

A character rotation by Alex Kirwan for *Call Me Bessie!*, a short created by
Diane Kredensor and Dana Galin for Frederator/Nickelodeon. Copyright
2008, Viacom International, Inc. All rights reserved.

animation experience. Kredensor, having worked in animation mostly as
a storyboard artist and supervisor, had never before created or produced a
pilot of her own. Kredensor explains, "So, I had absolutely no idea where
to begin or what the heck I was doing! My biggest challenge was to get
over that I didn't know what I was doing and just do it. Fortunately, I had
tremendous support and guidance from Fred Seibert, Eric Homan, and
everyone at *Random! Cartoons* and Frederator and Nickelodeon."

Kredensor created her pilot's storyboard as well as the initial designs,
and then hired designers to finesse those designs. She continues, "We
also hired a phenomenal director, Yvette Kaplan, whose timing is im-
peccable. During production, she actually started acting like the main
character in our pilot. My most important role was as a creator—to carry
our vision from A to Z and then empower an extraordinary team to do
what they do best."

While Kredensor brought in an outside animation director to helm
her pilot, as a storyboard artist and designer, she was integral to the visual
aspects of her pilot. Writer-based creators are even more dependent on
others to help bring alive the images in the writer's imagination. Adam
Peltzman reports, "Because I'm a writer, the biggest challenge was figuring
out the look of the pilot. I worked with a talented director and art director, both of whom helped a great deal by doing countless sketches of
backgrounds and characters, and through that process, a look slowly came
about. I'm not someone who can see every visual detail in my head, so
that collaborative process was key."

As a writer-creator, Peltzman defined his role by writing the pilot script and through involvement in hiring the key players: animation director, art director, voice-over cast, composers, etc. Peltzman explains, "Once the nitty-gritty of production started, much of the day-to-day work was handled by the animation director, art director, line producer, and supervising producer. My role at that point was mainly approvals—giving notes on the animatic, shots, voice-over records, and music."

Amy Steinberg not only co-created and co-wrote her pilot, she also served as one of the pilot's producers. "My primary responsibility was to give clear creative direction throughout the process," she says. "Since my sister and partner on this project, Liza, and I are not animators or designers, we worked with a design director and an animation director whom we completely trusted. My sister and I worked with them to establish the look of the show."

It's not uncommon for animation artists to work in many areas over the course of a career, and it's no different for creators. Janet Perlman says, "For our pilot I had to wear many hats, including producer, though I am primarily a creative person. We set up a production office specifically for this project. The hardest thing I found was to remain creatively involved in the pilot while things like financing, setting up the studio, and legal issues were tugging me away. I would avoid doing it this way in the future."

Debra Solomon finds that it's hard to find a happy medium in duties and responsibilities. She admits, "I know I tend to lean in the direction of doing too much directing so that the world I'm creating reflects my inner world. For *Private Eye Princess* I was director and script writer, and came up with the basic character designs. On top of that there was the day-to-day supervision of all the art that was churning out around me—supervision of the storyboards, script changes, color, props, and background designs. Doing all that alone is a big job."

Solomon advises other artists heading into a pilot to do whatever you can to avoid burning out: "Build in some time when you *have to* relax, sketch, work on new ideas, play with your cat, whatever . . . because once your brain crosses the, 'I can't do it anymore' line, your stress hurts the project and makes it less fun for everybody. It's important to remember that your mood sets the tone of every day on the project."

A good coping device might be for a creator to focus on his essential input or contribution. I recently saw a good example of a creator being spread thin by busy work that anyone else could have been doing. She

VIEW THROUGH THE VENETIAN BLINDS

In the private eye princess every day is so hot n' humid that the sweat runs down the pearl buttons on the back of your princess gown...down your sparkle tights, and into your Olympic sized shoes. The sorta day that you wish your puffed sleeves had central AC. But whataya gonna do? Fightin' crime and chasin' evil characters like Spanish dancer, Mr. Meenie, The Knight in Shining Armor and Rasputini, you work up a sweat. Maybe if you're bumbling enough ya fall into a body of water big enough to cool off. Maybe not.

All I know is that its up to me, the Private Eye Princess, to right the rights or wrong the wrongs...or something like that...cause crime just seems to happen when I'm around – maybe cause I'm a motivational force. Maybe just cause trouble is my business.

The title character page from Debra Solomon's pitch for her pilot *Private Eye Princess*. *Private Eye Princess*, its logo, and all related characters and elements are trademarks of and © 2008 The Cartoon Network.

was handling tasks such as coordinating meeting times and other unessential details. Once she realized the problem, she was able to delegate the uncreative daily tasks with which she had previously been burdened.

Navigating Network Development Notes

> "I went through more than five executives on my pilot, *Kenny and the Chimp.* There was massive turnover going on at Hanna-Barbera even before the merger happened, so I never knew whom I'd be talking to next. There was one that, I swear, had never seen a cartoon before ('How is it possible that Chimpy can take Kenny's nose off his face?'), and no matter how hard I tried, I couldn't get this exec to 'get' it. I eventually called to say that I was gonna take the project somewhere else, but the executive cut me off and told me [he was] leaving the company. So, I just said, 'Um . . . never mind.' In general, notes from the network can sometimes be very vague. You want them to tell you *exactly* what's wrong and *how* to fix it, but often they don't know what's wrong, they just know something's not right. It can really get maddening, especially by the sixth round of revisions."
>
> —**Tom Warburton, creator of *Codename: Kids Next Door* (Cartoon Network)**

The pilot may seem like the creator's golden opportunity, but it is equally a work for hire, made to a client's order. With that reality, it only makes sense that the network or Web destination that engages you to make a pilot will have some degree of creative input, especially since those in charge are supposed to be experts in the business of entertainment. A pilot is a commercial venture, and keeping this in mind can help you navigate the development of your pilot. That said, creators shouldn't automatically cave on every note. The creator was engaged for a unique vision, and sometimes it is necessary to battle in order to preserve the key aspects of that vision. But not all creative battles are equal; pick and choose carefully.

In the course of writing this book, I kept stumbling upon Web sites and blogs where artists described the development world as being filled with clueless executives living only to obstruct and destroy creators and their creations. While there are sad instances of this happening, it is far

Here's Lucy. Show art by Albert Truong for Loren Bouchard's *Lucy, Daughter of the Devil* pitch to Adult Swim. *Lucy, Daughter of the Devil*, its logo, and all related characters and elements are trademarks of and © 2008 The Cartoon Network.

from a universal truth. Besides, where does all this complaining get us? What do we learn from it? It would be far more constructive to focus on understanding how a healthy relationship between the creator and the network helps determine whether or not your pilot moves to series.

Adult Swim's *Lucy, Daughter of the Devil* creator Loren Bouchard provides a positive example of collaboration between a creator and a network by saying that, for him, communication with the network was smooth and easy: "The stereotypical image of that relationship—contentious, creatively stifling, etc.—seems way off base to me. Even notes that you disagree with have creative value. At the very least, they force you to defend your decisions and clarify your vision. More likely, they help you catch mistakes and improve your show."

As if to provide the polar opposite experience, another pilot creator tells me about her nightmare situation: "During our pilot's production, we got a lot of notes, which we always addressed in attempts to appease the network executive. Because they were asking for changes all the way through, it showed they didn't really get what our pilot was about. The problem was the executive [who greenlighted] our project left the network, and then the development mandate changed, putting our pilot out of favor with the new creative direction." All projects in development are similarly at risk. This author's development deal similarly fizzled out without even a changing of the guard, executive-wise. For whatever reasons, my executive and her network changed their minds midstream.

As a creator, I didn't see one opportunity as *the* opportunity. This allowed me to not take the rejection personally, which helped to preserve my good relationship with the executive and the network. Two weeks later the executive invited me to join a different project as a writer, proving that even when a project goes up in flames, it need not burn bridges.

Happily, shorts development programs such as Frederator/Nickelodeon's *Random! Cartoons* tend to offer a relatively light amount of creative notes. This may be in part because the emphasis of these initiatives is to throw a wide net and produce a large amount of shorts simultaneously. To expedite this process, these shorts programs tend to greenlight projects that are ready to go with minimum to no input necessary. Diane Kredensor agrees, "Before we started production, Fred Seibert told me that he was going to have minimal involvement. His philosophy was that we sink or swim on our own. That's really the only way he felt he'd know if you could actually run your own show/series in the future. Nickelodeon gave minimal notes also. I found many of their notes were good and I took the ones I agreed with and left the ones I didn't agree with behind. I felt that the communication between us and Nick and Frederator was really smooth, although I do believe I'm a great communicator, and you pretty much get what you give."

Creator Amy Steinberg had a much closer day-to-day collaboration with the network during her pilot's production. "We had weekly meetings with the network executives, during which they gave feedback on everything we had to show," she says. "The execs were hands-on without being overbearing. It was a great working relationship." Steinberg's pilot was produced in-house at Nickelodeon's New York City digital animation studio, where I was one of the animators. Digital in-house productions offer creator and client the opportunity to reshape a project during production, which sometimes results in unforeseen animation changes that can push a project over schedule.

In contrast, Kredensor's pilot's animation was outsourced overseas to South Korea, so the animation had to be planned out to the letter well in advance. Day-to-day changes that were common on Steinberg's pilot would be cost-prohibitive in Kredensor's model. There are pluses and minuses to both methods. The obvious minus to digital in-house production is that creators and networks can be noncommittal and endlessly fussy, resulting in a looser production that has a tendency to wear out its crew, while going over budget and over schedule. Outsourced pilots can suffer from a lack of spontaneity, being that all the creative aspects are locked into place from the moment the animation ships overseas. This gives outsourced pilots one chance to get it right, and sometimes one chance may not be enough.

Fran and Will Krause (co-creators and brothers) went through years of development and storyboard revisions at Cartoon Network prior to pilot production. For this reason, the network did not give a lot of notes during pilot production.

"If they've approved a pilot for production, most of their concerns have already been addressed," Fran explains. Overall, communication between the Krauses and the network was pretty smooth during production; however, he adds, "during development we had a few train-wrecks, mostly because we were calling between New York and L.A. and couldn't see where one another were pointing."

Teaming With a Production Studio

> "I met the founders of Fluid Animation (my pilots' and series' production studio) at the Geneva airport, en route to the Annecy Animation Festival. We connected because we were all confused about the shuttle buses."
>
> —**Loren Bouchard, creator of** *Lucy, Daughter of the Devil* **(Adult Swim, Cartoon Network)**

In the grand scheme of things, pilots are often down and dirty, fast and cheap productions. I'm reminded of an old Saturday Night Live sketch in which Kevin Nealon plots a bank robbery with the simple plan of "In and out . . . and nobody gets hurt."

Typically a pilot's length will be anywhere between two and eleven minutes, with pilot production contained to three to six months. Pilots made for networks, such as Nickelodeon, Cartoon Network, and The Disney Channel, are often produced at their in-house facilities, which are ready to tackle pilots and series orders as they arrive. "Nick Jr. commissioned me to pitch them a show concept," creator Adam Peltzman explains, "with the understanding that if the pilot was [greenlighted], they would use their studio to produce it. So it was all set up from the get-go."

The network studios expect pilot creators to work with some of the studio's own talent pool. Creators already working at studios are clearly at an advantage, having already formed relationships among the artists and production personnel.

An outside creator stepping in to make a pilot at one of the network studios may have a very different experience. Tom Warburton was one such outside creator. He says, "It was scary because I didn't know any of the artists in Los Angeles, so I had to blindly hire people, or I was forced to take people from the full-time staff; a good portion of whom (but certainly not all) did everything by rote and had long ago had their personal creativity beaten out of them."

"I still remember the shock on a colorist's face when I asked her what color she thought something should be. She stared back at me and said, 'You know, no one's ever asked me for my opinion before,' he recalls. "That kinda made me sad."

Being thrown into a new situation like this doesn't always turn out like Tom Warburton's first experience. Exposure to new artists and ideas can be very inspirational, helping to lift a creator and his project to new heights. And if proximity counts for anything, Warburton had ample opportunity to be influenced by a host of legends of animation past and present while working on his second Cartoon Network pilot in L.A. His office was right next to Bill Hanna's and a couple doors down from Joe Barbera's, which enabled him to rub shoulders with them almost every day. Additionally, he spent as much time as he could afford lingering around the floor where *The Powerpuff Girls* was being made. "I couldn't wait to meet Genndy Tartakovsky and Craig McCracken, two people whose shows were the reason I wanted to be on Cartoon Network," he recalls. Working at Cartoon Network in L.A. also afforded Warburton the opportunity to strike up friendships with *Billy and Mandy* creator Maxwell Atoms and *Family Guy* creator Seth MacFarlane.

The cartoon-producing networks also work with smaller independent studios to produce some of their pilots, particularly when a creator already has a relationship with such a production studio. Additionally, studios such as New York City's Curious Pictures create their own pitch projects, intending to act as their own production studios for any resulting pilots or series. Nowadays, pilots may also be produced by a small handful of people working out of their living rooms and staying connected via e-mail, instant messaging, phone, fax, and sharing work files through an FTP site.

Sounds Like a Plan

> "Our first pilot was very handmade; we did our own voices, music, all that stuff. In the second pilot, we decided to get some voice actors and some professional music, which also turned out to be a great help."
>
> —Fran Krause, co-creator of *Utica Cartoon* and *The Upstate Four*, Cartoon Network

Soundtrack is half the experience of a film, TV show, or Webisode. When it comes to the success of an animated project, proper casting and directing of voice talent can make or break the production. A character's voice helps solidify the character in the public's imagination (for example, SpongeBob's signature voice and infectious laugh, provided by Tom Kenny). In addition, since voices are recorded prior to the animation stage, they are the building blocks on which animators and directors create a performance. A dull and unemotive voice track won't inspire a crew of artists, and it's one thing that can't be fixed in post-production.

Authentic voices are charming, and this is important in casting voices for a preschool project. Creator Amy Steinberg explains, "When you're casting real kid voices for preschool shows, it's extremely important that you cast kids who can enunciate. It's also important to cast voices which are distinct enough to not be mistaken for each other." I would add that it's equally important to write *characters* that are distinct enough to not be mistaken for each other. This is particularly a problem in preschool content, an area in which I have spent much of my career. A key test in any preschool project might be to see what would happen if you swapped one character's lines with another. If such a switch makes little to no difference, then you haven't written distinct characters. This is a huge weakness in preschool programs, where most characters are defined by different degrees of cheerfulness.

Casting real children lends a project an automatic easygoing charm, but Steinberg cautions, "Working with kids is particularly difficult, because they often don't understand the voice-over process, and how tedious and demanding it can be. Finding kids who can focus and perform for long periods of time is no small feat." Although Diane Kredensor didn't enlist children to voice her characters, she too found that the most successful voices in her pilot were the ones that were the actors' natural voices.

Fran Krause and his crew of fellow animation cowboys did all the voices for their first pilot for Cartoon Network. "We're not good voice actors. We can only do deadpan. It fit the mood, but for the next pilot I put out a casting call on Craigslist and in *Backstage*. The response was huge, and we wound up doing twenty-four hours of auditions. It was a blast. I recommend having the voice actors bring in humorous monologues, rather than giving them dialogue to read. That way, you get to hear different things and don't get bored hearing the same lines over and over."

Nickelodeon's casting department helped Adam Peltzman set up the voice-over auditions for his pilot. Because he used only adult voices, he got to hear some of the top voice talent in the industry. Peltzman advises, "I think it's important to have a solid sense of what you're looking for and who your characters are—that gives the actors a better chance to come up with the voice you're looking for, and for you to know that voice when you hear it. That said, don't be too tied to any single voice in your head; you want to be open to surprising takes that you hadn't considered."

Loren Bouchard strays from the conventional wisdom, which decrees that you need to hold casting calls and auditions. "Walter Lantz said auditions are about the director's vanity and I tend to agree. You don't need to audition anyone. Good performers know other good performers. In this way, they're like bacteria—you find one and you can grow your whole cast from [that person]. I look in comedy clubs, and in particular, I look at sketch groups." Bouchard also advises, "Once you get their voices in your head, good actors will make you a better writer, a better animator, and a better director. My advice to creators and directors is to find talented performers who have interesting, likable voices, and never let them go."

Sketch comic and voice-over artist Becky Poole, who helped act out my final pitch to Frederator. She subsequently voiced pilots for Bill Plympton and Fran and Will Krause.

Along with voices, another key element of any soundtrack is the musical score, which can help tell a story in ways that visuals cannot. Music helps set the emotional mood, establish the time of day, and even bring out a character's personality. Music in animated film has come a long way since Walt Disney received credit for making the first-ever cartoon short married to synchronized sound (*Steamboat Willie*, 1928). In fact, when soundtracks appeared in early animated cartoons, they were doing what was referred to as "Mickey Mousing" because of their tendency to sync all the actions on the screen with accompanying music or sound effects. The result was a soundtrack that mirrored the animated motions of the characters on screen. Today, film scoring is an art form in and of itself. Scores and sound design can work in sophisticated ways, utilizing unconventional music and sounds that contrast or play around the visuals unexpectedly. One of the many innovations of John Kricfalusi's *The Ren & Stimpy Show* was the way he used vintage mood music tracks from the library of British production music company KPM to underscore his quirky series.

Since many series creators have musical talents as well, it's no surprise that some of them prefer to handle their pilot's musical chores themselves. Yet this is one decision that a creator should not make lightly. If you are truly the best choice to do the music for your pilot, then kudos to you. If there is any doubt, why leave such a key ingredient to chance?

Fran Krause, his brother, Will, and their animation crew did voices as well as the music and score for their first pilot. The indie score seemed to fit the handmade feel of the rest of the pilot. The brothers Krause had a different plan in mind for their second pilot: "I sent an e-mail to my favorite band, Beulah. They'd recently broken up, but their lead singer/songwriter Miles Kurosky was starting to write soundtracks and wanted to work on our project. He and another gifted musician, Nik Freitas, did amazing work on the pilot. I think there's only about twenty seconds out of eleven minutes that doesn't have music. They made about thirty separate songs. Basically, I just sent them a mix CD and asked that the music have a feeling like the songs on the CD. They did a great job." The killer soundtrack is just one of the charms of the Krauses' second pilot, *The Upstate Four*, and this was not lost on Cartoon Network executives, who promptly engaged the brothers to storyboard out another two episode ideas.

Tom Warburton agrees that it's always worth approaching your favorite musicians if you think their work could be a good match for your project. "I tried to get Pete Townshend for an episode and was roundly rejected . . . although I did get an autographed picture for my troubles. I did manage to get GWAR and The Upper Crust for episodes, which rocked pretty hard."

For the main scoring on all six seasons of *Codename: Kids Next Door*, Warburton enlisted Steve Rucker and Tom Chase because he'd loved their cinematic sound work on *Dexter's Laboratory* and *The Powerpuff Girls*. "Their hyper-talentenaciousness [*sic*] to do any genre, the speed at which they work, and most importantly, their ability to drive the emotion of an episode still blow me away," says Warburton.

Adam Peltzman asked a handful of different composers to write short demos based on a description of the pilot and some notes on what he wanted the music to feel like. Peltzman explains, "I think these notes were helpful to the composers in getting a sense of what kind of demo to put together. Choosing the winning demo was easy because one stood apart from the others as the freshest, most original sound."

Amy Steinberg employed composers with whom she'd already worked during her days on Nick Jr.'s *Blue's Clues*. "I knew that they were supremely talented, and that they'd nail the underscore. We didn't want to risk working with unfamiliar artists. The turnaround time was so quick that we felt it was best to stick with what we knew."

However you find your composer or musician, make sure you precisely communicate your vision for the music and sound. It would be quite a gamble to drop a pilot off to a composer with no instructions, or with the only directive being "surprise me." This is a risky proposition, even if you know the composer's work. Music and sound are as collaborative as any stage of a pilot's production, and a creator should champion her vision while staying open to new, appropriate ideas a composer might have.

The Role of Focus Groups

"My pilot sat in a drawer for a little bit, then it went out for market testing, where kids and parents behind two-way mirrors turned dials and told researchers what they thought of it. They seemed to like it, but not quite enough. So it went back in the drawer, and remains there today. A lot of pilots end up in that drawer and never get out. It seems like a pretty big drawer."

—**Adam Peltzman, creator,** *Monster News* **(Nick Jr.)**

Not only did Peltzman's pilot for Nick Jr. have to reckon with focus groups, it also had to compete against at least three other pilots for a chance to go to series. As Peltzman's story reveals, it did not get a series deal. Noggin creator Amy Steinberg's pilot was taken out for focus testing with preschoolers and their parents, where, she reports, "a comprehensive report was written, detailing everything from the appeal of the characters to the effectiveness of the curriculum."

Madeleine Lévesque, executive vice president of content development at 9 Story Entertainment, believes focus testing should only inform your decisions, not make your decisions for you. "If you have three pilots and you test them, clearly the one that tests the best will have the best shot at being [greenlighted] . . . but it may not be enough," she says. "We tend to forget that the breakaway hits always come from behind. *The Simpsons*, *SpongeBob SquarePants, Family Guy*—these shows tested terribly."

For a few years, Cartoon Network premiered its pilots in the "Big Pick Weekend." Fran and Will Krause's first pilot, *Utica Cartoon*, was featured in the weekend-long competition in which the viewing audience (not network-appointed focus groups) voted to pick which short might go to series. Although the kids didn't pick *Utica Cartoon*, Cartoon Network executives liked the Krauses enough to work with them again. "They liked *Upstate Four*, which we just finished up last fall. I think some focus-group kids said they wanted to see more of the boy characters (there are three boys and one girl) so we're writing two additional storyboards with more of the boys." A network and a creator can use this kind of feedback to make revisions to a project in hopes of getting a pick-up.

Tom Warburton had the rare experience of being present during a focus-group test of his first pilot. He recalls, "At the time, Terry Kalagian was the head of focus testing for Cartoon Network. We watched the kids from behind the one-way glass, and she could tell who was who just by looking at 'em. 'That kid's the alpha male. He'll say something and the other kids will all agree with him. The girl next to him? Nice Catholic girl. She won't like professor XXXL because he's mean to Kenny. The boy next to her? He'll be picking his nose in T-minus three seconds.' And she was dead-on with everyone."

Cartoon Network's Adult Swim remains the only successful block of (mostly) animated programming targeted to men ages 18 to 34. Rival networks might want to take note that Adult Swim does very little focus testing, if any at all. Creator Loren Bouchard explains, "Instead, I think

Don't make her angry. You wouldn't like her when she's angry. A still from Fran and Will Krause's second pilot for Cartoon Network, *The Upstate Four*. *The Upstate Four*, the logo and all related characters and elements are trademarks of and © 2008 The Cartoon Network.

they rely on a combination of informal screenings, hallway discussion, and internal lobbying. When my pilot for *Lucy, Daughter of the Devil* wrapped, it went through this internal process pretty quickly. The verdict was that it had promise, but they wanted to see some scripts before they committed to a series. So, they paid us to write six scripts. We also eventually recorded and produced the audio track for one of these scripts as a kind of second, audio-only pilot. It was based on this audio that they [greenlighted] the series."

Development has often been described as a moving target. While networks have their creative mandates to guide them, the sheer length of time required to make a pilot sometimes means that the winds change before a pilot's completion. Debra Solomon reports that by the time her second pilot was delivered to Cartoon Network, it was clear that a cartoon with a woman—rather than a young girl—was not going anywhere.

"The AOL Time Warner deal was going south, and while Cartoon Network was supportive and great," she says, "*Private Eye Princess* was not going to be a show. And the era of shows targeted only to boys was back in full force."

These trends are forever in motion, so it's a game to try to predict which way the wind might blow next. Who would have guessed that the wind would blow in the direction of an undersea cartoon about a square, yellow sponge? Maybe networks should leave studying the wind to the meteorologists.

Post-Mortem

"If I were going to do anything over again in the *Lucy, Daughter of the Devil* pilot process, I would ask for even more feedback. That's tough to do when you're working hard and you're tired and you're in love with your show. But I think sometimes network executives will hold back significant concerns, especially if they're hard-to-articulate worries about look and feel, or concept. If your goal is to get a series you're gonna want to hear those worries sooner rather than later."

—**Loren Bouchard, creator of** *Lucy, Daughter of the Devil* **(Adult Swim, Cartoon Network)**

With so many factors adding up to create—or sabotage—a pilot, it's no wonder that creators can readily name which battles they lost and at what cost lessons were learned. Loren Bouchard's story poses what might be considered a creator's ultimate challenge: not only addressing notes but being open to notes and collaboration as well as actively seeking that feedback. If network executives hold back their notes, they can take the creator completely by surprise at a later stage. "When we finished the *Lucy, Daughter of the Devil* pilot, we were very happy with the result and we expected it to go right to series. But it didn't," Bouchard recalls. The network's concerns had been withheld partly because of Adult Swim's policy of extending a large amount of freedom to creators. "It's a mixed blessing, as Mike Lazzo (executive vice president at Turner Broadcasting, in charge of Adult Swim) says. They give you enough rope to hang yourself. In retrospect, I wish they'd been a little harder on us at the pilot stage," says Bouchard.

Sometimes factors affecting a pilot aren't even from outside forces. As a first-time creator, Diane Kredensor struggled to find her voice early in the production process. "As a consequence, I'm not 100 percent happy with some of the early choices that were made on our pilot. One of those was in voice casting and directing. I rushed to a decision in picking one of the voices and didn't direct them powerfully. I would most likely recast if we go to series."

As artists, we often have an idea or vision of the finished product in our heads that can't possibly come to complete fruition. Usually, there is a point where a film starts to take on a life of its own, guiding its creator to make specific decisions on a day-to-day basis. Kredensor confesses that in some ways the pilot exceeded her expectations and in others she was slightly disappointed. "Visually, I'm very proud of the outcome and thankful for the amazing talent I had to help bring it to where it is," Kredensor says. "I was a bit disappointed that the writing came across much younger than we initially intended. My co-creator, Dana, and I both have a simple, silly sense of humor, and it translated as very young. That's not necessarily a bad thing, it's just not what I intended."

Some surprises can be prevented by thorough early planning. Adam Peltzman wishes he had a clearer idea of what he wanted his end product to look like. Researching various preexisting art styles at the start of a project can present some directions for a designer to run with. It may sound like an obvious thing to do, but once you're ensnared in production and managerial issues, you may not have the time or inclination to consider all the design possibilities at your disposal. The Internet makes searching for visual inspiration easier than ever before. And thumbing through children's magazines, comics, and animation trade magazines can give you a good idea of what styles are hot at the moment. You may end up borrowing a bit from here and there to make something new, or, at the very least, you may discover what you don't want, which can be just as useful.

Another problem new creators face is trying to put too much into the pilot, which is understandable considering the effort you've put in to get your pilot in the first place. You want it to showcase everything you've dreamed of. But this could backfire on you. "The pilot doesn't need to introduce every aspect of what the series will be; it just needs to be a solid stand-alone piece," says Peltzman. "I think I may have loaded too much story and too many characters into my pilot in an effort to show it all."

This is one of the hardest things of all to get right in a pilot. How much of the total series plan should you introduce in a pilot? There's no set answer, but you'll probably want to include enough hints of a larger world without being crushed by the weight of it. A rule of thumb is to focus only on what you can fully explain or do justice to without detracting from the core elements (the characters, conflict, and world) that need the most attention. The ideal pilot should be like a random, great episode of your series-to-be. It shouldn't shoulder the burden of enacting all the situations or character combinations that might occur naturally over the course of an entire season of episodes.

Most often, pilots have very concrete deadlines set by the network or production studio, which can create problems beyond your control. "Some of the mistakes I made on the previous pilots can't really be avoided unless I have some more time," says Fran Krause. "I can manage

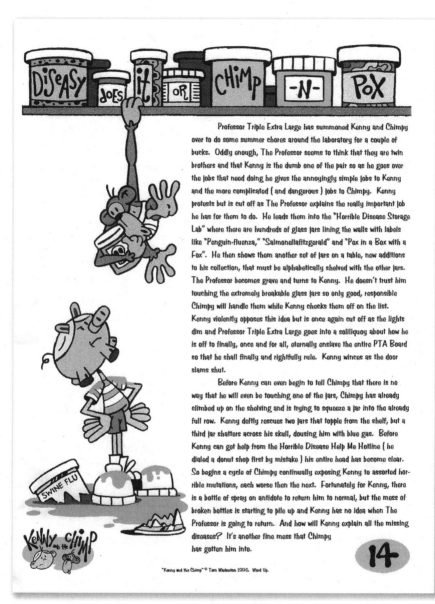

Professor Triple Extra Large has summoned Kenny and Chimpy over to do some summer chores around the laboratory for a couple of bucks. Oddly enough, The Professor seems to think that they are twin brothers and that Kenny is the dumb one of the pair so as he goes over the jobs that need doing he gives the annoyingly simple jobs to Kenny and the more complicated (and dangerous) jobs to Chimpy. Kenny protests but is cut off as The Professor explains the really important job he has for them to do. He leads them into the "Horrible Disease Storage Lab" where there are hundreds of glass jars lining the walls with labels like "Penguin-fluenza," "Salmonellafitzgerald" and "Pox in a Box with a Fox". He then shows them another set of jars on a table, new additions to his collection, that must be alphabetically shelved with the other jars. The Professor becomes grave and turns to Kenny. He doesn't trust him touching the extremely breakable glass jars so only good, responsible Chimpy will handle them while Kenny checks them off on the list. Kenny violently opposes this idea but is once again cut off as the lights dim and Professor Triple Extra Large goes into a soliliquoy about how he is off to finally, once and for all, eternally enslave the entire PTA Board so that he shall finally and rightfully rule. Kenny winces as the door slams shut.

Before Kenny can even begin to tell Chimpy that there is no way that he will even be touching one of the jars, Chimpy has already climbed up on the shelving and is trying to squeeze a jar into the already full row. Kenny deftly rescues two jars that topple from the shelf, but a third jar shatters across his skull, dousing him with blue gas. Before Kenny can get help from the Horrible Disease Help Me Hotline (he dialed a donut shop first by mistake) his entire head has become clear. So begins a cycle of Chimpy continually exposing Kenny to assorted horrible mutations, each worse then the next. Fortunately for Kenny, there is a bottle of spray on antidote to return him to normal, but the mess of broken bottles is starting to pile up and Kenny has no idea when The Professor is going to return. And how will Kenny explain all the missing diseases? It's another fine mess that Chimpy has gotten him into.

14

A story summary from Tom Warburton's pitch bible for *Kenny and the Chimp*, which became the basis for the story of his first Cartoon Network pilot. Note the wall of text, which the creator avoided in his subsequent pitch bible for *Codename: Kids Next Door*. *Kenny and the Chimp* and *Codename: Kids Next Door*, their logos, and all related characters and elements are trademarks of and © 2008 The Cartoon Network.

my pilot's time better if I can hire an animation director to help out next time around, but who knows what my budget will be?" Time is always shorter than we like on any given stage of production. In the medium of pilots and series, it is important to know when good might be good enough. At some point, creators have to let some little things slide so they can focus on putting out bigger production fires.

Tom Warburton's second pilot may have led to the hit Cartoon Network series *Codename: Kids Next Door*, but that doesn't mean he's above a little Monday morning quarterbacking on his two pilots: "It was a bit of a shock to me that neither *Kenny and the Chimp* nor *Codename: Kids Next Door* looked anything like *Star Wars*. But does any project really turn out the way you envisioned it? By the end of each pilot, I was so burnt, so tired of looking at them, all I could see were things I wanted to fix—things no one in their right mind could ever see unless they had spent 167 years (or what felt like that) making it. I think it took me at least a year before I could look at either pilot and say, 'Hey, that's not so bad.'"

A recurring theme of this book is the importance of a creator developing and pitching ideas that are close to his heart. A genuine passion for your subject is necessary if you expect your best work to come out. Debra Solomon, creator of three pilots to date, agrees: "I think if I work on a pilot again it will be closer to the view in my independent films. I have no idea who the hell would want to do a pilot about infertility, as in *Everybody's Pregnant,* or someone trying to get over a broken heart, as in my recent project for HBO, *Getting Over Him in Eight Songs or Less*, but I intend to find them. At first glance that may seem to be a rarefied audience, but really, it is a female-centric audience. I will try to keep all my future work closer to my areas of interest: sex, dating, love, and hate . . . sounds like fun!"

Chapter 10

Launching the First Season

"Keep in mind that making a pilot and making a series are two different things. Making a pilot is like tossing a ball into the air and making a series is like juggling fifty balls at once."

—**Craig McCracken, creator,** *The Powerpuff Girls, Foster's Home for Imaginary Friends* **(Cartoon Network)**

Y̲ou may have noticed by now that this book's primary function is not to impart a business plan or give step-by-step instructions on how to budget or schedule a pilot or series. Fear not: there are others who have already written those books, which are conveniently listed in this book's appendix. Our focus here is on how to best utilize production to get the creator's vision on the screen.

In the case of launching a first season, this means expansion of ideas, process, crew size, and an increase in challenges you'll face. The trick when starting any new animated series is to avoid trying to reinvent the wheel. The old models worked fine in their time and a lot of those systems still apply today and can be adapted to production in the digital age. All productions start with a series order, a budget, a schedule, a crew list, computer/software requirements, and the network or Web destination's deliverable final format specifications. All workers must be given ap-

Art by character design supervisor Shannon Tindle for Craig McCracken's *Foster's Home for Imaginary Friends*, which won the artist an individual achievement Emmy Award for outstanding character design. *Foster's Home for Imaginary Friends*, its logo, and all related characters and elements are trademarks of and © 2008 The Cartoon Network.

propriate resources of time, equipment, and supervision to complete their tasks within the set schedule. All work and workflow must be numbered, tracked, delivered to the hand that needs it next, and eventually assimilated into an archive library for subsequent reuse. All creative notes and revisions coming from sources both internal and external must be organized and addressed.

You probably won't be reading this chapter while poised to launch a first season of your own, so as a would-be creator, imagine this chapter's contents as a series of "good problems and challenges to have."

Crewing Up

Some years back, a couple of friends of mine formed their own animation studio, which they founded after landing a major client that supplied fairly steady work. The partners' long history in the business meant that they had no trouble recruiting a talented group of familiar friends and colleagues to help handle the work. Slowly the pair began to notice something—some of the "friends" took advantage of the situation and acted less professionally than they might if working for a relative stranger. Gradually, these first freelancers were replaced with fresher talent that truly relished the relationship as well as the work.

While it's not always so, friendships can bring unhealthy baggage. I can attest that in my first years as a director, more often than not, the difficult employees were either friends or people with whom I had previously worked as equals or peers on the same series. In contrast, new hires were brought on who knew me only as a director or boss. They were often ready to work hard and were excited to collaborate with me. Unlike my friends and former coworkers, the new hires didn't try to test me or use friendship as an excuse to behave in an unprofessional manner.

I don't mean to suggest that friends will always let you down as employees. This is far too general an assumption to make. While directing animated series for several different studios, I've had a hand in staffing decisions, sometimes—as in Adult Swim's *Assy McGee*—with the authority to choose my entire crew. Eight out of nine of my hires on *Assy McGee* were people I had previously worked with and each of them I would call a friend. (In fact, one of them happened to be my father.) Sure enough, the one employee that didn't work out on this series turned out to be one I hadn't worked with before. However, friendships should not be the only (or even the most important) criteria to use when staffing.

A creator who has worked for years in the industry has the opportunity to pull in his favorite artists, and preferably ones he's worked with before or who at least come highly recommended by trusted individuals. Tom Warburton explains, "The general idea when staffing a show is to hire people who are better than you, which was easy in my case." I fully appreciate what Warburton is saying. While at *Blue's Clues*, I got to see a great example of this in action. Over the course of the first season of the show, co-creator (and de facto art director) Traci Paige Johnson passed along her vision to Christian Hali and Ian Chernichaw, who both went on to head the show's art department. As the *Blue's Clues* art department expanded, Hali and Chernichaw continually raised the bar with each hire, bringing in stellar artists such as Astrid Riemer, Amanda Lattrell, and Jennifer Palmer so that by the series' end, Traci Paige Johnson was heard

A still from *Bob and Margaret*, co-created by Alison Snowden and David Fine (Snowden Fine Productions and Nelvana Limited). © 2008 Nelvana, Ltd.

to remark, "At this point, I wouldn't be qualified to work in the art department of my own show!"

Tom Warburton explained to my SVA career class that over years of working in the industry he made a mental list of all the people he would love to hire in the event that he was ever in the position to do so. "When *Codename: Kids Next Door* got greenlighted to series, I was very lucky in that there was a dry spell (work-wise) here in NYC. So, I got to hand-pick all these phenomenal artists like Gideon Kendall, Guy Moore, and Matt Peters. I knew them and knew their work, so I knew they'd be perfect for the job," says Warburton. Other artists on his mental list were people he hadn't worked with but always wanted to, such as Kim Arndt, Todd Myers, and Anthony Davis, all of whom he brought aboard his crew.

A mental list such as this works both ways. Over a period of years, you take stock of all the people you encounter and note those you would not hire. Warburton suggests you think about staffing the way you'd think of inviting people over to your house for a really long party. "I'll take an okay artist with a great attitude over a hyper-talented jerk any day."

Another staffing challenge is that just because you get along with someone who is a terrific artist does not automatically qualify him to work in every show's aesthetic. I've personally experienced frustration working with some talented 2-D animators who happened to be fantastic draftsmen but couldn't properly translate those skills when animating in a limited way with a Flash or AfterEffects puppeted character. No matter how diverse our skills may be, none of us is the right fit to work in every possible animation style. *Bob and Margaret* co-creator David Fine concurs, "Doing a show of this scale, there were inevitable problems with some whose style didn't work for this kind of show. Occasionally, we would have a great deal of redoing to do, and that put a lot of pressure on us and the production."

The Delicate Art of Collaboration Between the Creator and Network

Agreeing to make a pilot, film, or series with a network is agreeing to give the network a say in how you do it. They aren't putting up the money for nothing. Not everyone is cut out to make a short cartoon for mass consumption, let alone a series. According to Tom Warburton, there are a lot of compromises, aggravating opinions, and flat-out fighting that go into it. "If you can't handle that, then make a short film of your own where you can do it your way and if it's great and fits the mold, the networks will come to you," he says. To this I will add that even then, the network will want a say.

There's a belief held by some creators that development executives and networks ought to get out of the way once a show goes into series. In their misguided fantasy, once the network cuts the check, its role is over. "If they bought an idea from you, then that means it's an idea they like," says Butch Hartman of *The Fairly OddParents.* "But now that they've paid you for your idea, it becomes *their* idea, too. They're paying for it, so they have a lot of say in the matter."

The truth is that development does not end once a show goes to series.

As a pilot's scope is expanded to a longer episodic format, there is a lot of new development. A good example of this is John R. Dilworth's *Courage the Cowardly Dog* series for Cartoon Network: in the original short, *The Chicken From Outer Space,* the dog didn't speak at all. "In fact, nobody spoke," explains Dilworth. "In the series, I wanted to have the dog talk . . . and we tried it. If you see the first half of season one, Courage does a lot more talking than in the whole series, and it really was Cartoon Network that encouraged me not to have the dog talk. We limited his talking to screams, babbling, and whines—and it works. That was a great call."

Dilworth's story shows how the collaboration between creator and network is supposed to work. In the ideal situation, creators and development executives work together on finding the right balance to create the best product possible. The executives will always have something to add, which is their job. "And a lot of times, they're right and have very good advice on how to make an idea more marketable," says Butch Hartman. However, there are some times when the development executives get a little too involved and try to change the idea completely. When this happens, Hartman advises, "Even though you don't know everything and neither do they, you've got to do your best to stick by your original vision."

Dilworth, like most veteran creators, can cite experiences with networks where things did not go smoothly. The real problem can be personality clashes, which is why it so important for both creators and networks to do their best to put egos aside so they can get down to work. "I think it's all ego. We don't like to be told what to do," says Dilworth. "We don't like to have our ideas challenged. We want to be able to express ourselves."

Sometimes, development executives will try to butt into areas outside their training. When this happens, creators need to choose their battles. "I like to stay open to the network's needs, but I usually call foul if an executive (who went to law school) starts art-directing my show," says Doug TenNapel, creator of *Earthworm Jim* and *Catscratch*. "There is no such thing as a singular vision intact on a television show. Executives either get behind the creator or get in front of him."

The worst development executives are often ones who are secretly frustrated creators themselves. The proper role of development executives is not to remake your show their way, but to gently guide, enable, and empower you to produce your vision. PBS's Linda Simensky adds, "The best development executives, I think, need to be interested in turning the creators they work with into stars." Additionally, Simensky recommends that development executives also check their ego at the door, suggesting that when you work in development, you have to remember that it's not about you, it's about the shows you find; and that starts with the creators you discover and nurture. When a creator gives in on every note that comes his way, it demonstrates his insecurity or lack of faith in his own talent or voice. Similarly, if a development executive feels the need to dominate the creator, it demonstrates her insecurity or lack of faith in the very creator she chose to produce the project. Teletoon's Athena Georgaklis believes that its important for a network to take a respectful position and try not to overpower the creator, because the show needs to be driven by the people who know it best.

"Developing a show is a long process with lots of chances to get frustrated. Remember that you will be judged on how you react to those frustrations. If a creator openly says what is bothering him, then great," says Heather Kenyon. "We can do something about it and attack the problem head on together. All too often, we hear through the grapevine that someone is upset or the person will get angry, be passive aggressive, etc. And this then will make us wary. How will they act when they are halfway through season one and the schedule is slipping and their main voice actor is moving out of the country and their favorite director just got stolen away by a competing show?"

The first season of any series is rife with challenges, and creator of Nickelodeon's *Hey Arnold!*, Craig Bartlett, points out that it might be "where a series can get noted to death." An unending flood of major notes coming from the network can mean something other than a strained relationship between the network and the creator. It could indicate that a series is fatally flawed and ripe for cancellation after delivery, especially if the ratings don't immediately deliver the goods. In 2005, a network abruptly canceled its unfinished, unaired series after constant notes delivered amid season one hindered production to such an extent that very little work was accomplished or approved. The result was the layoff of an entire production crew on a day's notice.

Another troubled series at another network barely survived into a second season, which, upon delivery, was dumped in an awful time slot nobody would be watching. The show's development executive confided to me that they knew something was wrong with the show when they had to keep giving so many notes throughout the series' run. By most accounts, the creator's ego was a major factor in allowing the show's creative problems to drag on so deep into production.

Finally, Jerry Beck, creator of Frederator/Nickelodeon's *Hornswiggle*, provides what might be the secret to finding a balance between a network's notes and a creator's vision, suggesting that the creator delicately try to steer all the executives' notes toward her own ideas. Beck concludes, "I find it a fun challenge to accept a network change and try to make it work in a way that satisfies me. It can be done."

Production Challenges

"I don't think you ever know what it will be like until it's on top of you . . . and then you swim. You just keep swimming."
—John R. Dilworth, creator of *Courage the Cowardly Dog* (Cartoon Network)

The challenge of producing an animated episodic series is also its own reward. On any series, even in the best circumstances, money and time are never in the amounts a creator desires. The treadmill of the assembly line is always turning, limiting the amount of time and attention you can lavish upon any one section or stage. The challenge of the animated episodic series is that it attempts to mix art with commerce. For example, there's not one correct way to lay out any sequence of action. More than one way might work, but certainly we might wind up with the best way if we have the correct creative staff in place, working within an efficient organization that helps remove any obstacles in the way of their success, even as the assembly line is forever ticking forward.

Jackson Publick (Cartoon Network's *The Venture Bros.*) explains, "Time and money are the biggest challenges, as always. They're both limited, and they both keep you from being able to keep revising and embellishing and finessing your work." Publick suggests that this, however, can be a good thing because it forces one to become more confident in making decisions and to use all resources as efficiently as possible. Animation legend Ralph Bakshi calls this "respecting production," which translates into: budgets and deadlines are sacred.

The Ren & Stimpy Show is a good example of what can happen if the production's artistic needs surpass the limits of time and money. In that example, the network notoriously stepped in and ousted the creator after there was friction between the two parties stemming from disagreements over the level of violence and controversial content in the series, as well as woes over missed deadlines. The fact that this marked the beginning of the end for the series proves that the relationship between art and commerce must be symbiotic for the venture to survive and thrive. Without the artist or creator's vision, the show is doomed to be a soulless corporate product. Too much artistic control without any regard for time and budget may cause commercial consequences that close the door on the artist or creator's opportunity.

Since episodic animated series have been in existence for decades, making schedule and budget while making sure the creative is taken care of should be no mystery. Nickelodeon's *SpongeBob SquarePants* creator Stephen Hillenburg puts forth an overall creative philosophy: "keep it simple." To achieve this, he and his crew look for humor in simple situations (that eventually reach absurd proportions). "We put the characters together and watch what happens . . . you know, like red ants and black ants. We are only doing eleven-minute stories, so there are not a lot of subplots," Hillenburg says.

Another production problem might be geography, which was certainly a hurdle Tom Warburton had to overcome before his series could get off the ground. He explains, "Cartoon Network actually sent me out to L.A. to make my two pilots. *Kenny and the Chimp* (my first pilot) was the first Cartoon Network/Hanna-Barbera/Warner Brothers hybrid after their big merger and was quite the crazy experience. No one was really sure who was supposed to do what since there were so many jobs crossing over between the companies. But it went as well as it could and I had some great people helping me . . . and I discovered In-N-Out Burger. Mmmmmmm."

Creator Tom Warburton toasts with an exotic beverage in a plastic cup at the 2006 Ottawa International Animation Festival. Photo by Amid Amidi.

A couple of years later, Warburton's *Codename: Kids Next Door* pilot came right in the middle of Cartoon Network's move to its Burbank, California studio. "When my show eventually got greenlighted to series, Cartoon Network really wanted me to do the show at the studio in Los Angeles. But after a World War 7–like battle, I was finally allowed to do the show in NYC. I think what finally convinced them was [that] my wife designed knitwear and there wasn't much of a sweater business out in L.A. (and they weren't paying me enough to scuttle her career), [that there was] a lull in the business here in NYC (so I could hand-pick the best people I knew to work on my show), and that I was working as a director on *Sheep in the Big City* at Curious Pictures," says Warburton. *Sheep* had just been canceled and had a really great production pipeline already in place, so if Warburton did it there, Cartoon Network knew they could get the show done on time and on budget.

On my recent job directing season two of Adult Swim's *Assy McGee* for the Boston-based studio Clambake Animation, our biggest challenge was how to structure the workflow to meet the needs of a unique production model. Like most productions, we started with scripts, storyboards, and animatics. But unlike other productions, the writing could change significantly between each stage and continue changing from there. Whole sections would be rewritten after presenting the rough cut of the animation, and still more might be rewritten even at the fine-cut stage. In truth, this always led to marked improvements in each episode. But such a process requires additional time and money, and this affects the schedule. By our fourth episode, we were weeks over schedule. With only so many hours in a day, my animation artists and I had to jump back to revise and reanimate sections of older episodes, which meant less time to spend working on a new episode. Less time on a new episode meant there would be more late revisions on it, and so on.

I knew something was wrong when my role became "the guy who says no." I was the animation director, not someone who should stand in the way of what, with some fine-tuning, might be a unique and successful creative production process. Clambake and I knew the situation could not continue without some readjustment to the production process. In the end, some employees had their contracts extended. More importantly, we arrived at the decision to delegate the time-consuming animation revisions to artists working internally at Clambake, thus freeing up my offsite animation crew to focus only on delivering rough cuts for each episode. Right away, we began to catch up, and our strained pipeline and stressed-out crew were able to function much better. The rest of the season, which was the majority of the episodes, went very smoothly once we had all learned our production lessons.

Productions should not try to reinvent the wheel when it comes to creating a system or a pipeline to handle animation production, but, inevitably, every show is a little different. Even with the best production plan, there will likely be bumps to smooth out along the way. Smart productions react swiftly to any challenge. I was impressed at the speed with which the producers of the series *Pinky Dinky Doo* reacted to a hiccup in its production flow. The supervising director on the series, Jeff Buckland, and the episode directors, J. P. Dillard and myself, noticed a problem created by our first pair of episodes as they passed through production. We had too many assistant-level animators and not enough lead animators. The assistants finished their work quickly, and the lead animators were bogged down and running behind in delivering finished animation.

Executive producer Melanie Grisanti and producer Tina Moglia swooped in to make solving this problem a priority. Ultimately, we decided to promote our four best assistant animators to junior lead animator positions so they could handle some of the finished animation, which greatly took the pressure off our overworked lead animators and allowed us to hit our show deliveries. The remaining assistant animators still blazed through their work quickly, so J.P. and I found creative ways to keep them busy and motivated by assigning them simple animations and lip synch. The remaining production went smoothly.

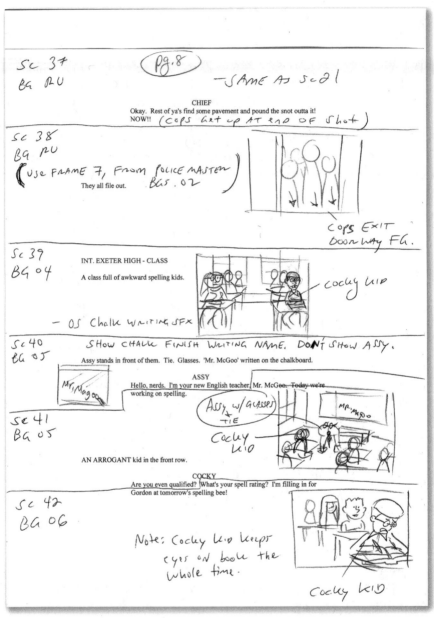

Sc 37
BG RU

Pg.8

— SAME AS sc 21

CHIEF
Okay. Rest of ya's find some pavement and pound the snot outta it!
NOW!! (cops get up at end of shot)

Sc 38
BG RU
(USE FRAME 7, FROM POLICE MASTER)
They all file out. BG5. 02

COPS EXIT
DOOR WAY FG.

Sc 39
BG 04

INT. EXETER HIGH - CLASS

A class full of awkward spelling kids.

Cocky KID

— OS chalk WRITING SFX

Sc 40
BG 05

SHOW CHALK FINISH WRITING NAME. DON'T SHOW ASSY.

Assy stands in front of them. Tie. Glasses. 'Mr. McGoo' written on the chalkboard.

Mr. Magoo

ASSY
Hello, nerds. I'm your new English teacher, Mr. McGoo. Today we're
working on spelling.

Assy w/ glasses
TIE

MR. MAGOO

Cocky
KID

Sc 41
BG 05

AN ARROGANT kid in the front row.

COCKY
Are you even qualified? What's your spell rating? I'm filling in for
Gordon at tomorrow's spelling bee!

Sc 42
BG 06

Note: Cocky KID keeps
eyes on book the
whole time.

Cocky KID

A sample of the author's director sketches from an episode of Adult Swim's
Assy McGee. *Assy McGee*, its logo, and all related characters and elements
are trademarks of and © 2008 The Cartoon Network.

The secret shame of production challenges is that all too often, they go unsolved. This generally means the same outcome for any show: the employees are made to bear the brunt of bad planning and decisions from the top. On such productions, employees say goodbye to evenings and weekends because employers expect them to devote additional hours to delivering shows that are built on unreasonable production models, created and sustained by creators and producers who don't have the skills or knowledge or patience to figure out better models. At one such studio in New York, a young crew objecting to the mandatory unpaid overtime rallied together and presented a petition to management, after which management stood down. Animation artists and production personnel have the potential to wield an amazing amount of power to improve even the worst-case production models at the most clueless of studios, even in a non-animation-union city such as New York.

However, this author makes the assumption that you represent the reasonable and well-intentioned creators, studio runners, and producers, who (thankfully) make up the majority in this industry. The only agenda a producer or supervisor should have is to remove any obstacles that take away from giving the creative staff maximum creative time and energy on each and every episode. Good production plan aside, one should never forget that, at the end of the day, it is *people* who are responsible for any project's success.

In-House Digital Production Versus Utilizing an Overseas Studio

Economic considerations factor highest in the decision of whether to produce a series in-house or to outsource it to an overseas studio. It's a sign of the times that we are even asking this question. From the late 1970s onwards, the default method of animated TV series production was to outsource the time-consuming and expensive animation stage of production overseas, most often to South Korea, where there was a large, experienced, and inexpensive workforce eager to do the jobs. This model of production left pre-production duties in North America, which included scripts, voice tracks, character/background/props design, storyboards, animatics, and exposure sheets. The exposure sheets provided a frame-by-frame set of instructions for the overseas animator to follow. Finished animation would arrive back in North America, where the domestic crew would perform post-production duties, among which were editing the picture together to a rough cut, calling retakes, locking the picture, scoring and mixing of sound, and outputting to final delivery format.

This TV animation episodic production model went unchallenged until the 1990s, when three successful digitally animated in-house productions (Mainframe's *Reboot,* Nick Jr.'s *Blue's Clues,* and Comedy Central's *South Park*) paved the way for TV series animation jobs to return to North America. Today, in-house digital animation production is plentiful and most often utilizes animation production in Flash, AfterEffects, or Maya (and sometimes creative combinations of all three). In-house digital animation is perfect for animation with simpler graphic styles where there is not a lot of frame-by-frame drawn animation required. As a result, it's not surprising that in-house digital production has made the deepest inroads in three areas: preschool series TV; Cartoon Network's Adult Swim lineup; and most Web-based cartoons where animation and art needs are usually not too heavy.

There are many benefits to digital production that is fully in-house. First off, writers, producers, directors, designers, storyboard artists, animators, and editors have a chance to learn from each other as they work together under one roof. This greatly increases the chance for good communication and the development and implementation of shared work procedures, which should benefit a project artistically as well as help keep it on schedule and on budget.

It's amazing how crew members can come together and push and inspire each other on to excellence. There's a natural healthy competition that happens. *Blue's Clues* supervising director David J. Palmer would recognize one especially outstanding "shot of the week" every week at the show's animation department meeting. All animators benefited from analysis of the outstanding work, and many of them aspired to be the subject of next week's acclaimed animation. The importance of this in-house training and recognition technique became apparent as our off-site animators began to be left further and further behind the growing standards of excellence. This just goes to show that having an in-house creative team allows for a more effortless approach to communication and training. Palmer's innovative "shot of the week" program was part of a larger creatively enriching production culture set down by *Blue's Clues* co-creators Traci Paige Johnson and Angela Santomero, who continued to foster happy productions on their subsequent shows, *Blue's Room* and *Super Why!*

David J. Palmer with animators Trevor Woolley and Keelmy Carlo, showing just how competitive *Blue's Clues'* shot of the week became. Or maybe this photo was taken on Halloween. Who's to say? Photo from the author's collection.

In Leslie Iwerks's documentary *The Pixar Story*, the studio explained that one of the secrets to its creativity is to encourage "unplanned collaboration." This is yet another benefit of in-house production because animation artists or technicians might arrive at the solution to a problem through spontaneous interaction and teamwork.

I was recently part of a newer production model in which the crew was an equal combination of onsite and offsite workers. With his business partners Andre Lyman and Carrie Snyder, Carl W. Adams opened an animation studio, Clambake Animation, to tackle the second season of *Assy McGee*. He was in need of an animation director, so Adams met with me for lunch in New York City so we could sniff each other out as potential collaborators. I had just bought an apartment in Brooklyn and was not looking to move to the Boston area (where Clambake is located). In the past, and under normal circumstances, this would be a deal-breaker, but with modern technology, I was able to propose an arrangement to Clambake that would be mutually beneficial.

As a new company, Clambake was not readily able to afford the number of computer workstations needed to tackle a series. Nor would its management be able to easily staff an entire animated production using the Boston-area talent pool, which is largely tied up working for a small handful of existing studios in that city. The answer? My proposal was that they allow me to augment their staff with a team of contractors working under my supervision from Brooklyn while I directed the series from my living room. That is exactly how we proceeded and (once we smoothed out a few kinks) it worked swimmingly, or should I say, "Adult Swimmingly?" The off-site crew reported to me via phone calls, e-mails, and instant messaging, and I was able to attend important staff and production meetings at Clambake through video conferencing. All of us uploaded and downloaded work to and from a common server accessible through Clambake's FTP site. As I write this, post-*McGee*, Clambake and I have already repeated this arrangement, tackling animated spots for Sesame Workshop's *The Electric Company*.

The right people working in reasonable systems under supportive supervision is what will allow any crew to go above and beyond both creative and production expectations.

The Creator's Role on a Series

Earlier in this chapter, development executive Linda Simensky gave this advice to her fellow development executives: "When you work in development, you have to remember that it's not about you, it's about the shows you find, and that starts with the creators you can find and nurture." Not only do I wholeheartedly agree with Simensky, but creators can use similar advice: "It's not only about you and your opportunity, it's also about how you communicate your vision and collaborate with a team and professionally nurture each and every one of them to contribute their very best."

Generally, creators have three important basic responsibilities. The first is as an employee providing a service. For example, if the creator is also the head writer, then she will write a heavy percentage of the scripts and supervise the contributing writers. Nickelodeon's *Hey Arnold!* creator Craig Bartlett reports, "Every series is different. I concentrated on the story aspect and was most involved at the beginning and the post-production parts of each cartoon. I love making the cut, being responsible for getting each show to length. And the sound mix is always fun, I never miss it."

In addition to writing scripts, creators might provide series-wide or episode-specific services of an art director, voice director, animation director, supervising director, and so on. However, creators should not get carried away and try to work in areas outside their expertise. One recent series (which derailed at the starting gate) owed part of its problems to its producer assuming the role of art director, a position far outside of his reach. His inability to do the job helped cause endless design problems and revisions, which in turn caused delays in production and squandered the show's resources. Ultimately, key financial backers decided to pull the plug on the series, resulting in the mass layoff of seventy-five employees on a day's notice. Sometimes we need to realize, as Stephen Hillenburg did in hiring talented artists to help him create illustrations for the *SpongeBob SquarePants* pitch bible, that although you may be a capable artist, you may not be the right artist or director to make your show its best.

The next responsibility a creator has is to communicate the creative vision on a series to a crew and to delegate work and responsibilities. *Pinky Dinky Doo* creator Jim Jinkins warns that creators shouldn't get bogged down in the details at the expense of the creative. "My role is to make sure the show is staying creatively on track by staying involved in the daily process. I delegate now more than ever," says Jinkins. "It comes from cultivating relationships with artists and producers [whom] you work well with and share a mutual sensibility and ethos."

For Adult Swim's *The Venture Bros.* creator, Jackson Publick, delegating some of his responsibilities meant first and foremost splitting the writing duties, which he says "was weird at first but always yields pleasant surprises. On that side of things, giving the characters over to the hands of someone capable, talented, and funny has reshaped the show, because half of the shows are coming from someone else's perspective. Our sensibilities can be incredibly similar sometimes, and where they differ, my show reaps the benefits of a whole different dimension. A lot of [co-writer] Doc Hammer's work has changed the way I write, too. We kind of build off each other. And of course, it helps to have someone you're both collaborating with and, in a friendly way, competing with, because you try to get better and better at cracking someone up."

"I have to delegate the work, obviously, but obsessing over details and such is part of what I enjoy about it. If I know exactly how I want some-

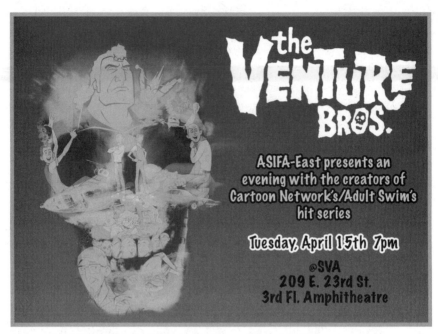

A poster heralding ASIFA-East's evening with the makers of Adult
Swim's *The Venture Bros.*, which included panelists Liz Artinian, Stephen
DeStefano, Jackson Publick, and Doc Hammer. Organizations such as
ASIFA-East offer introductions to some of today's top talent. *The Venture
Bros.*, its logo, and all related characters and elements are trademarks of and
© 2008 The Cartoon Network.

thing to look or move or sound, I'm going to push for it," says Publick. "If
I don't know what I want, that's where the artists get to be creative. And as
with any good, new thing coming into the project, it gets assimilated and
informs the next thing after it—it inspires you."

The final responsibilities of the creator are to provide leadership,
encouragement, and inspiration. Mistakes are allowed, even on the
creator's level of responsibility. Not learning from mistakes, however,
can result in loss of employees, a series cancellation, and even long-term
damage to the creator's reputation, which could block further successes. A
creator should facilitate solutions, bridge any communication gaps among
the team members, and, most importantly, help build a process without
obstacles or bottlenecks.

The creator also needs to avoid being an obstacle. For some, this
means learning to put ego aside. This can be tougher than it might sound.
A large ego might be a key reason why the creator got where she is today.

It's been said that just because one has the ability to create and sell a show doesn't make him well suited to run a production. Some creators have insecurities that prevent them from delegating key responsibilities that might lead to a smoother pipeline. In one extreme example I know, the creator insisted on being present for every stage of the process, which not only caused a jam in the process, but also required his employees to work late hours while they waited for his availability and notes.

This officious fellow erroneously believes that workers are dispensable. In fact, he's notorious for replacing an entire crew at the start of each new season of episodes, although it should be said that he only prevents half the crew from returning—the other half often elects to find a job with more stability. Such creators can be simultaneously brilliant at public relations but see no problem flooding the industry with disgruntled former employees. The long-term result cannot be in the creator's favor.

Success Beyond Success: Now What?

Just because a creation goes to series does not ensure a smooth career ride from that point on. In addition, once you are the creator of your own series, it might be difficult to imagine working for somebody else afterwards. This can be problematic simply because there are few individuals with more than one series creation to their name. Still another problem is that, as creators become known for their series, they may find themselves typecast within the industry, forever associated with one type of show.

Jim Jinkins looked up one day and saw that he was considered a preschool show creator because of *PB & J Otter*, *Stanley*, *Allegra's Window*, and *JoJo's Circus*. "I think the responsibility falls on my shoulders to make things that break the stereotype," Jinkins says. He's not alone in his concern. Craig Bartlett similarly answers, "As the creator of *Hey Arnold!* I am considered 'soft.'" To break away from that stereotype, Bartlett pitched a show called *Hellville*, which takes place in Heaven and Hell (Heaven being like a weird cult, and Hell being sex, drugs, and rock and roll). "I send that script out so people won't stereotype me," says Bartlett.

In addition to the creator's task of trying to break her own mold, self-promotion is another key to continued success in the industry. While self-promotion is important to any career in animation, most individuals don't capitalize enough on their successes. But not everybody looks upon self-promotion in a positive light. A few very shrewd self-promoters from

A still from Bill Plympton's Oscar-nominated *Guard Dog*. The filmmaker
is also a master of self-promotion, which can be a key survival skill in this
business. Image courtesy of the artist.

the world of independent animation sometimes invoke the ire of others
who frown upon this as "selling out." These prolific indie filmmakers
make it a point to create a new independent film nearly every year. Then
they expend just as much energy traveling to film festivals around the
world, where they compete for awards on the world stage. At the film
festivals, they also mingle with other filmmakers and meet potential
distributors and agents. Each film and festival trip is another salvo of
self-promotion and helps ensure that these filmmakers land lucrative
commercial accounts that in turn help pay for their next films.

Self-promotion is a key survival skill for all animation artists, not just
the superstars of the independent scene, and it need not be or appear
seedy or undignified. Unfortunately, there are people who reinforce the
worst attributes of self-promotion. One producer has accurately described
another studio operator as the type of person who would display a fake
Emmy on the mantel. This same operator includes a misleading biography
in his press materials, which claims him as the "creative force" behind
another creator's hit series when, in fact, in his role as producer, he made

no creative contribution to the series. Another line from the same biography boasts past work as an animator at one of the world's most prestigious animation studios. In reality, he preformed entry-level tasks on minor television work at a satellite company affiliated with the large prestigious studio. Anybody who perpetuates such falsehoods in self-promotion will be looked upon with suspicion, disdain, and dismissal by the animation community.

In the same way independent animators utilize self-promotion, the creator in development with a pilot/series production can use her time as a networking opportunity. In the world of pitching and development, time under contract for development is an avenue to propose subsequent projects, thus exploiting your status as a successful creator. One hit series creator took time to travel to film festivals, where he was a featured panelist on industry discussions. Festival travel brought him into contact with rival network development executives, one of whom signed this creator's next development deal. He might not have had such a smooth transition to this subsequent opportunity without the time invested in self-promotion.

You don't have to be a creator of a hit series to enjoy a similar benefit to your self-promotion. Everyone in animation, with or without a development deal, should make time to stay connected to others in the industry. It's important to make new connections as well. For more advice and ideas on networking, check out the networking chapter of my book *Your Career in Animation: How to Survive and Thrive.*

What does a creator of a successful series want next? What gift do you give to the "man who has everything"?

The answer to both questions is socks. They are practical and nobody can ever have enough of them.

All kidding aside, a creator who has one series to his name has no guarantee that another will follow in its wake. If he wants to break through again, he should have a stockpile of new ideas to follow up the current project. Some creators may set their sights on other challenges (feature films, novels, screenplays, etc.) once they've conquered an episodic animated series.

Mo Willems, the creator of Cartoon Network's *Sheep in the Big City*, had a very successful animation career and created an original character series for Sesame Workshop and for Nickelodeon before he set his sight on children's books. Today, you can't walk into a bookstore without

Mo Willems's *Leonardo the Terrible Monster*, now a best-selling book as well as an award-winning animated film directed by Pete List. Image from the book *Leonardo the Terrible Monster* by Mo Willems. © 2005.

encountering Willems's very successful line of children's books, which have brought him a level of success far beyond even his acclaimed work in animation. Oddly enough, Willems's success in children's books has led him back to animation, as Scholastic/Weston Woods has been adapting the author's books into animated films, with Willems functioning as his own producer. The first two of these films, *Knuffle Bunny: A Cautionary Tale* and *Leonardo the Terrible Monster* have already begun to cut an impressive trail through film festivals worldwide. Willems's friend and colleague Tom Warburton has followed up his impressive six-season run of Cartoon Network's *Codename: Kids Next Door* with his own children's book deal.

There's no doubt that previous success will open doors for us, even if we seek to put our energies toward areas other than animation pitching and development. I recently read an interview in *Bust* magazine with *Juno* screenwriter Diablo Cody, in which she outlined her upcoming slate of projects. It was truly an impressive example of success breeding success. Striking while the iron is hot, Cody was working under contract to write several movies and TV series simultaneously, showing that one way to extend success is through sheer productivity.

The challenge of following up a successful animated series is the ultimate example of a "good problem to have," and may it be yours to solve soon enough.

Chapter 11

Happy Trails: Parting Thoughts and Advice

"Don't put all your eggs in one basket. Develop several ideas and set up multiple meetings with rival networks. Keep busy and don't wait around for any one meeting to respond. Keep creating things that would be fun to see . . . and fun to work on."

—Jerry Beck, creator of *Hornswiggle* (Random! Cartoons, Frederator/ Nickelodeon)

I started my career as a creator peddling his wares by pitching some station identification spots to MTV animation. In that case I had followed the development executive's advice and mailed my pitch ahead of time. A few months later, I was able to arrange an in-person meeting with the executive to get some feedback on the proposal. Imagine my surprise when, at the start of the meeting, the executive admitted he had lost the materials. The good thing about an origin story like this is that there's nowhere to go but up. As a sidebar to this story, shortly thereafter, this same executive became the talk of the town after he decided to demonstrate a karate chop in a development meeting with a creator and her lawyer. That display ended in a trip to the hospital and numerous stitches, happily confined to the karate master himself. The creator's project died in development as they so often do.

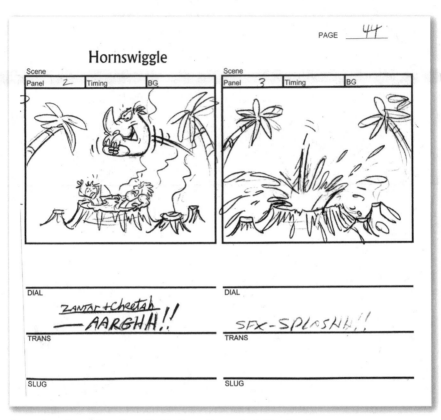

PAGE 44

Hornswiggle

Scene			
Panel 2	Timing		BG

Scene			
Panel 3	Timing		BG

DIAL

ZANTAR + Cheetah
—AARGHH!!

TRANS

DIAL

SFX - SPLASH!!

TRANS

SLUG

SLUG

A storyboard page from Jerry Beck's short, *Hornswiggle* (Random!
Cartoons), drawn by Tom Sito.

After ten years of pitching without so-called success, it's a natural
thing to take stock of one's journey. A natural place I keep coming back to
is a quote from independent animator Patrick Smith used earlier in this
book: "I see many talented artists working very hard pitching shows all
the time. If they funneled that kind of energy toward making a film, they
might have a little something more to show for it."

I don't have to wonder what I had to show for the energy I expended
on pitches. As of 2004, my pitches had started to produce a different kind
of success, albeit one that didn't end directly in a development deal, pilot,
or series. That was the year Fred Seibert and his Frederator partner Eric
Homan began to dangle a series of carrots in front of my face, helping
to rekindle my interest developing cartoon pitches. A test pitch-film I
made that same year, with animator Dale Clowdis, didn't secure a TV

Tara Sorensen, vice president of development, National Geographic Kids Entertainment. A couple of years after I first pitched to Sorensen and her department, they engaged me to direct a pilot for a new series. It's rewarding that even when pitching doesn't end in a greenlight, it can still turn into the beginning of mutually beneficial relationship.

deal, but instead helped score me a great job directing on Jim Jinkins's preschool series *Pinky Dinky Doo*. Rounding out that year, a fluke book pitch to Allworth Press resulted in the greenlight to author my first book, *Your Career in Animation: How to Survive and Thrive*. Here was a pitch that scored a direct hit the first time out. This unexpected success helped level off my disappointment when a yearlong round of invited pitching at Frederator didn't produce fruit.

A short time later, I began to pitch the stockpile of projects I'd developed for Frederator. One of those pitches brought me back to Nickelodeon, where I was spontaneously pulled into a meeting by producers Claire Curley, Wendy Harris, and Marcy Pritchard and offered a job as the supervising animation director of the second season of Nick Jr.'s *Blue's Clues* spin-off series *Blue's Room*. In the same year, a slew of pitches via e-mail and conference calls to the National Geographic Channel Kids Entertainment division served as an introduction that capped off with a job to direct a pilot for them three years later, which was followed by a subsequent offer to help write/develop another series.

In 2007, friendships made via years of pitching (and bonding over the Beatles) with development executive friends Linda Simensky and Khaki Jones helped lead to my next job: directing season two of Cartoon Network's Adult Swim series *Assy McGee*. The adult-oriented series was a creative shot in the arm that resulted in the formation of my first original pitch for the same audience (I'm only now just beginning to shop it around).

The same week I accepted the job on *Assy McGee*, Allworth Press greenlighted my second book proposal, starting me on the path to write the book you hold in your hands. Best of all, in an astounding three-pieces-of-good-news-in-the-same-week scenario, my latest pitch proposal, after being rejected by at least five networks, scored a development deal at a major network. As I mentioned in chapter 8, "The Option or Paper Development Deal," I had written five episode scripts for the property before the network opted not to proceed to pilot. Only days after the development executive dropped the bad news, she recommended me for a development/writing opportunity on a brand-new preschool series. It was a chance to help write a show from the ground up and show off my preschool chops, which had first been formed under the tutelage of *Blue's Clues* creators Traci Paige Johnson, Angela Santomero, and Todd Kessler.

When you stay in the game for ten years, you notice some things. Development executives come and go (virtually none of the development executives are still in the same place they were in 1997). Fads, trends, and network development mandates change, rise, and fall. Windows of opportunity forever open and close. As a would-be creator, you have no control over any of the fickle, frustrating attributes of this industry. Your own desire to develop your talent, to persevere even when the odds are against you, and to contribute your voice to the mix are the only things you can count on.

The creators and development executives who lent advice to this book wouldn't dare let you leave without some final advice. Won't you join me in sending them each a mental high-five as a token of our appreciation? It might be awkward if the mental high-five finds them in the shower, but that's not our problem.

Creative Advice from Creative People

> "Some of the best animation creators were storyboard artists. If you aren't a strong storyteller, find someone who is that you work well with and collaborate with them. A design isn't a character. It's just the covering. The show needs a good foundation to succeed. I just always try to do something that entertains myself. I can't really second guess what others will like. But when pitching your show idea, you do have to think about what kind of shows are on a particular network, what age their audience is, and what their overall sensibility is. Then you figure out where your sensibility and theirs overlap."
>
> —Carl H. Greenblatt, creator of *Chowder* (Cartoon Network)

"Start with execution. I personally believe in artists, not ideas. Ideas are cool and all, and you can get really excited about them, but if the artist doesn't have what it takes to pull off their [sic] vision, the idea is wasted. I've seen good ideas go bad and 'meh' ideas blow me away all because of how great the execution was."

—Craig McCracken, creator of *The Powerpuff Girls* and F*oster's Home for Imaginary Friends* (Cartoon Network)

"There's sooooo much stuff out there, it seems impossible that you'll ever make anything, ever. If it wasn't for the fact that those things are filled with 99.9999999% crap, I would have given up hope before I'd ever pitched a show."

—Mo Willems, creator of *Sheep in the Big City*, Cartoon Network

"I've found a lot of inspiration from the successes of other independent creators: anyone who starts with something small and personal and new and strange and makes some mark in popular culture. Whether it's Klaus Nomi or the Blue Man Group or Quentin Tarantino or Michael Moore or Daniel Clowes or Chris Ware or a stand-up comedian or a band or a documentarian."

—Jackson Publick, creator, *The Venture Bros.* (Adult Swim, Cartoon Network

"Creativity is easy. It's overrated. Don't let any artist ever try to fool you into thinking it's hard. Digging ditches? That's hard. Fighting in Iraq? That's hard. Doing ten pull-ups on the playground, that's hard. But we open our mouths and creativity falls out. In fact, I'm looking for the tap that turns this creative crap off so I can get some sleep."

—Doug TenNapel, creator of *Earthworm Jim* and *Catscratch*

"One of the questions I always get from students is, 'I have an awesome idea for a show. How do I get it made?' I have to

Tom Warburton monkeys around with a fun page of poses for *Kenny and the Chimp*, his first pilot for Cartoon Network. *Kenny and the Chimp*, its logo, and all related characters and elements are trademarks of and © 2008 The Cartoon Network.

be brutally honest with them: You won't. Not now, at least. A network isn't going to give a kid with no experience a couple million bucks to make a show. Craig McCracken once told me that you had to work on someone else's show before you can have your own, and he was 2,000 percent dead-on. Graduate from school first and then go get a job on a show (I know . . . easier said than done). Start at the bottom and pay attention to every facet of production. Work your way up so when (and if) you do get your own show you know what you're talking about. You can't lead a team if you don't know how a production is run. That's not to say that a student shouldn't pitch his show idea. Go for it and learn from the experience. Maybe you'll even get to make a short. Just don't expect to be handed a series right out of school."

—**Tom Warburton, creator, *Codename: Kids Next Door* (Cartoon Network)**

A still from *Bronk & Bongo* (Random! Cartoons), co-created by Manny Galan and Alan Goodman. Copyright 2008, Viacom International, Inc. All rights reserved.

"I watch a lot of TV, and I'm a really easy audience, I basically can watch almost anything and like something about it (even if it's just enjoying how bad it is). From that, I might end up getting inspired or hooked on something that I see or inspired by watching actors and comedians that I really like. Sometimes it's easier to maybe write something with them in mind regardless [of whether] I end up using them or not. But I think it helps me by knowing what each network is about and it also just gives me ideas (or inspiration). At the same time it's too daunting to think of an idea being a series on TV. So I usually like to just think in terms of a little short that I think is funny or interesting."

—**Carl W. Adams, co-creator, *Assy McGee* (Adult Swim, Cartoon Network)**

"Open any issue of *KidScreen* magazine and you will no doubt be bombarded by the visual assault of half-baked and poorly executed ideas attempting to take advantage of current trends in hopes of having the next Dora, Ninja Turtles, or what have you. Trying to think about what you could do that would fit these trends consciously is fighting the natural creative process. Creativity should be allowed free reign to grow and flourish into whatever it may be, and at a certain point, the idea will take on a life of its own. It informs you what it is, how it works, and what the parameters of this world are. If you go about it trying to fit it into a mold of what is expected in terms of trend, your idea will carry the stink of insincerity."

—Manny Galan, co-creator, *Bronk & Bongo* (**Random! Cartoons, Frederator/Nickelodeon**)

"It is vitally important to maintain healthy working relationships with execs because they're the ones who can say 'yes' or 'no' to your project. Just be yourself and be open to their thoughts and suggestions, no matter how much you may or may not agree or disagree. If everyone can work together and drop the egos for a second, a great project will be made that everyone can benefit from."

—Butch Hartman, creator of *The Fairly OddParents* and *Danny Phantom* (**Nickelodeon**)

"I think everyone who wants to create a cartoon should try to make their own short to get the ball rolling. Your own short reveals your sense of art, story, timing, humor, and tone. It tells much more than just pitching your idea ever could. Make a short!"

—Craig Bartlett, creator, *Hey Arnold!* (**Nickelodeon**)

Dispatches from the Desk of Development

"When you go in to pitch, use it as an opportunity to sell yourself as a creative person. If the development executive tells

you the project isn't for their production company or network, instead of trying to change their mind, ask why. I have to say no if the project doesn't fit the goals that we have. Therefore, if you hear what we are seeking, it will help you come back next time with a project that is hopefully better suited."
—**Heather Kenyon, development executive**

"A pitch longer than fifteen minutes means the show is too hard to explain. Pretend that you have to tell someone what the show is on a ride to the fifteenth floor in an elevator."
—**Brown Johnson, president of animation, Nickelodeon**

"You can get a rejection fairly quickly, but constructive feedback takes time. If several people are going to look at an idea, and someone is going to put some notes together, it can take a while. Also, the higher up the executive is in the company, the more time it will take to hear back from them [*sic*]. I tend to look at projects in relation to each other, and that adds time to the process. It is okay to call or e-mail and check on the status of your project, as long as you don't start to nag. You might get a faster answer if you pose your question as, 'I am curious to know what you thought,' as opposed to, 'Please give me an answer as soon as possible.'"
—**Linda Simensky, vice president of children's programming, PBS**

"Get to know all the players involved, from the audience to the producers to the distributors, across all platforms. The era of developing a TV show as an isolated element is over. We are developing media that kids will experience across multiple screens as well as off screen. The more you know about the world in which kids are growing up and how media impacts their lives, the more effective you will be."
—**Alice Cahn, vice president, social responsibility, Cartoon Network**

"I think one of the biggest problems that I encounter from animators pitching for funding from Atom is not understanding our audience. I get a fair number of pitches that skew too young. Go to the site and check out the most popular animations (the top-reviewed pieces, etc.) to get a sense of our audience. We have an 18–34-year-old demographic, and so do many of our competitors. Also, many of the pitches feature episodes that run too long. Ten minutes or even seven minutes per episode is really too long online. I'm looking for one to three minutes per episode, because that's what the online audience will watch."

—Megan O'Neill, vice president, acquisitions and production, Atom Films

A Final Word from the Author: Perspective

Our best approach is to treat pitching and development as an exciting adventure and not rely on its success as the summation of a life's work or worth. Something recently reminded me of that the hard way. I had pitched my latest preschool idea to Nick Jr. (the same project was eventually picked up and then dropped by another network). The meeting hadn't gone too well, and that surprised me because I believed it was a very strong pitch. I agonized for weeks over how to respond. I decided to draft a friendly reply letter that addressed all of their creative notes and concerns and offered solutions and a new spin on my proposal.

On one evening while I was filled with anguish over sending out this e-mail, my father called with bad news: my mother, who had been a cancer survivor for more than thirty years, was back in the hospital—and this time, things looked grim. I felt sick at how wrapped up I had been in this minor little pitch. My mother died a few short weeks later, and I dropped out of all my work responsibilities for six weeks as my family came together to grieve and pick up the pieces. The frivolous little pitch was out of my mind completely.

I don't share the above personal story to say that pitching (or work, for that matter) is a meaningless pursuit. Our jobs and careers are a part of our lives for better or worse. My mother was very proud of my accomplishments and I was very grateful for her unwavering support and encouragement. Pitching and development are rewarding and stimulating

A tender moment from my film, *Good Morning*, which helped me reconnect with my muse shortly after the loss of my mother.

parts of my creative life, but they do not represent the most important aspects of my life. Who knows what the future holds, but one thing is certain: when I reach old age, I'll be able to say that I went after my dream. (Although by then, I might have a new dream—like having a full set of teeth.)

Appendix: Animation Pitching and Development Resource List

Organizations

Joining and volunteering for these organizations can expose hopeful creators to like-minded individuals as well as other industry-related professionals, veteran creators, and network development executives.

ASIFA-East

ASIFA is The International Animated Film Society (association internationale du Film d' Animation). It was formed in 1960 by an international group of animators to coordinate and increase worldwide visibility of animated film. ASIFA-East is the predominant Eastern United States chapter of ASIFA, based in New York City. ASIFA-East holds monthly screenings of animated films and publishes a monthly newsletter filled with information of interest to those in the East Coast animation community as well as fans of the medium. ASIFA-East also conducts a yearly animation festival, a unique showcase for the most groundbreaking independent and commercial animation being produced in the industry today.

ASIFA-East c/o Michael Sporn Animation
35 Bedford St., New York, NY 10014
www.asifaeast.com

ASIFA-Atlanta

ASIFA-Atlanta is the Southeast chapter of ASIFA. ASIFA-Atlanta sponsors free screenings of difficult-to-find animation, holds regular meetings to plan screenings, and features an annual "Roll Yer Own" screening every November, at which all members may screen their work.

ASIFA-Atlanta
410 Candler Park Dr. #B3, Atlanta, GA 30307
http://master.asifa-atlanta.com

ASIFA-Hollywood

ASIFA-Hollywood is the Los Angeles–based chapter of ASIFA. Since 1972, ASIFA-Hollywood has hosted an annual awards ceremony to honor individuals who have made significant contributions to the art of animation. The Annie Awards are regarded as animation's highest honor, and the ceremony is one of ASIFA-Hollywood's most prestigious and elegant events. Members participate in the nomination process and final voting.

ASIFA-Hollywood
2114 Burbank Blvd., Burbank, CA 91506
www.asifa-hollywood.org

ASIFA-San Francisco

With over 300 members ranging from seasoned professionals to students and fans, ASIFA-San Francisco is the Bay Area chapter of ASIFA. Membership in ASIFA-San Francisco provides monthly events and screenings, including an annual career night with leading animation houses, such as Pixar, ILM, Wild Brain, and PDI; annual open screenings, festival screenings, other special events; and a monthly newsletter focused on the Bay Area.

ASIFA-San Francisco
P.O. Box 14516, San Francisco, CA 94114
www.asifa-sf.org

ASIFA-Canada

The Canadian chapter of ASIFA. ASIFA-Canada members receive two to three issues of *ASIFA-Canada* magazine, $30 vouchers redeemable at the Ottawa International Animation Festival, free admission to ASIFA-sponsored screenings and events, and a membership directory (including animation studios, governmental organizations, and a list of all ASIFA-Canada members). Student ASIFA-Canada members (with ID cards) receive an additional $10 off the festival's student pass rate.

ASIFA-Canada
C.P 5226, Ville St. Laurent, Qc. Canada, H4L 4Z8
www.awn.com/asifa-canada

NOTE: There are other ASIFA chapters in different cities across North America. I have only listed above the largest chapters where there are the largest amounts of animation industry.

The Animation Guild Local 839 (TAG)

The parent organization of TAG is IATSE (the International Alliance of Theatrical Stage Employees, Moving Picture Technicians, Artists and Allied Crafts of the United States, Its Territories, and Canada, AFL-CIO, CLC). IATSE represents those involved in animation and CGI as well as representing "below-the-line" film contributors such as camerapersons, sound technicians, editors, live-action storyboard artists, set designers, art directors, scenic artists, etc. in the southern California area.

The Animation Guild Local 839
4729 Lankershim Blvd., North Hollywood, CA 91602-1864
www.mpsc839.org

Women in Animation

Women in Animation (WIA) is a professional, nonprofit organization established in 1994 to foster the dignity, concerns, and advancement of women who are involved in any and all aspects of the art and industry of animation. WIA is a networking organization that provides opportunities for members to meet and exchange business cards with interesting and influential people in the animation industry. Through WIA's workshops, meetings, and panels, members are bound to gain valuable insight into the industry, opportunities available to them, and other educational resources in their areas. With most members concentrated in the United States and Canada, WIA's influence and reach into many other countries are growing all the time.

Women in Animation, Inc.
P.O. Box 17706, Encino, CA 91416
www.womeninanimation.org

Women in Children's Media

Women in Children's Media (WICM) is an association of women who are committed to creating and distributing thoughtful, entertaining media to children and young adults. WICM builds connections, promotes professional development, and inspires our members to lead, innovate, and shape the future of children's media. Women in Children's Media affords its members opportunities to make a difference, hone their professional skills, stay on top of the job market, tap into industry events, and shape our legacy as the future leaders in the children's media industry.

Women in Children's Media, Ansonia Station
P.O. Box 231480, New York, NY 10023
www.womeninchildrensmedia.org

Web Sites and Blogs to Know About

My day has not officially started until I've had a cup of coffee and checked my favorite Web sites and blogs, which provide up-to-the-minute news, reviews, and information on the industry. I hope you allow some of the sites below to become a part of your morning ritual.

Animation World Network

The Animation World Network (AWN) is the largest animation-related publishing group on the Internet, providing readers from more than 145 countries with a wide range of interesting, relevant, and helpful information pertaining to all aspects of animation. AWN, covering areas as diverse as animator profiles, independent film distribution, commercial studio activities, and CGI and other animation technologies, as well as providing in-depth coverage of current events in all fields of animation, gives its readers an easy-to-navigate, visually and intellectually creative mechanism to electronically access a wealth of information previously unavailable anywhere in the world.

www.awn.com

Michael Barrier

Michael Barrier is the author of *Hollywood Cartoons: American Animation in Its Golden Age* and *The Animated Man: A Life of Walt Disney*. His site includes commentary on current films, books, and comics.

www.michaelbarrier.com

Cartoon Brew

A daily animation blog run by animation historian Jerry Beck (The Animated Movie Guide) and animation critic Amid Amidi (publisher of *ANIMATION BLAST*). Beck and Amidi do reviews, news, and commentary on all things animated.

www.cartoonbrew.com

Cartoon Research

Jerry Beck's online depository of all things related to classic Hollywood cartoons. It includes a database of all animated feature films released in the U.S.; pages devoted to rare images from Warner Brothers, Fleischer, MGM, and Terrytoons (among other studios); and a FAQ that answers common animation history questions.

www.cartoonresearch.com

Frederator

A collective of eclectic blogs themed around the business of Fred Seibert's production company, Frederator.

http://frederatorblogs.com

John Kricfalusi

The energetic blog of *The Ren & Stimpy Show* creator John Kricfalusi.

http://johnkstuff.blogspot.com

David B. Levy

This author's weekly animation blog, called Animondays, which reports on the industry and art of contemporary animation with an emphasis on the New York City area. Updated (you guessed it) every Monday.

http://Animondays.blogspot.com

Mark Mayerson

Reflections on the art and business of animation from an animator, writer, producer, and director of TV animation for over twenty-nine years, Mark Mayerson.
http://mayersononanimation.blogspot.com

Jackson Publick

The journal of *The Venture Bros.* creator Jackson Publick.
http://jacksonpublick.livejournal.com

Michael Sporn

Academy Award–nominated animator/director Michael Sporn's informative daily blog.
http://michaelspornanimation.com/splog

Doug TenNapel

The informative musings and goings on of *Earthworm Jim* and *Catscratch* creator Doug TenNapel.
http://tennapel.com

Mo Willems

Your one-stop location for all things by Mo Willems, including a blog, a FAQ section, and much "Mo" stuff.
http://mowillems.com

Trade Publications

Arriving like a present in your mailbox, these following magazines provide an ample survey of the animation industry's past, present, and future.

ANIMATION BLAST

ANIMATION BLAST, a purely independent magazine in print since 1998, is "not subservient to the studios" and doesn't regurgitate their press releases. *ANIMATION BLAST*'s group of contributors includes Jerry Beck, David Calvo, Greg Duffell, Will Friedwald, Shane Glines, Mark Mayerson, Aaron Springer, and Gabe Swarr. *ANIMATION BLAST* is the brainchild of publisher/editor/author Amid Amidi.
   www.animationblast.com

Animation Magazine

The magazine dedicated to the business, technology, and art of animation.
   30941 West Agoura Rd., Ste. 102, Westlake Village, CA 91361
   (818) 991-288
   www.animationmagazine.net

Hollywood Reporter

The monthly magazine and online content that allows one to stay connected to what's happening in the entertainment industry.
   www.hollywoodreporter.com

KidScreen Magazine

The leading business publication in the world serving the information needs and interests of kids' entertainment executives. Published nine times a year, *KidScreen* is delivered to 13,000 kids' entertainment decision-makers around the world.
   www.kidscreen.com

Variety

For breaking entertainment news, movie reviews, celebrity photos, pictures, entertainment industry events, film festivals, festival news, and festival reviews, etc.
   www.variety.com

Festivals

Although some warn not to mix business with pleasure, the two seem to blend quite nicely at the animation-oriented festivals listed below. Attendees have the opportunity to mix and mingle with filmmakers, animation artists, creators, development executives, and industry types of all stripes.

Animation Block Party

Animation Block Party is dedicated to exhibiting the world's best independent, professional, and student animation. The mode of broadcast is always evolving, be it through Internet streaming on the Animation Block Party Web site, free screenings for the public, official Animation Block Party festivals, or DVD distribution. The Web site homepage also offers three Web selects every month for mass consumption.

www.animationblock.com

The ASIFA-East Animation Festival

For more than four decades, the jewel of ASIFA-East has been its animation festival, which is the longest-running annual animation festival in the world. It appeals to professionals and novices alike and is casual enough for students and veteran animators to mingle, discuss, and toast the subject they love best—animation. In this age of home video, digital cable, and the Internet, ASIFA-East brings live bodies together through the festival. Friendships, partnerships, and businesses have been sparked from the ASIFA-East connection.

www.asifaeast.com

The Chicago International Children's Film Festival

The Chicago International Children's Film Festival (CICFF) is North America's largest and most celebrated film festival devoted to films for and by kids, and it's the only Academy Award–qualifying children's film festival in the world. The Festival welcomes more than 26,000 Chicago-area children, adults, and educators to hundreds of screenings. More than

100 filmmakers, media professionals, and celebrities attend the festival to lead interactive workshops with kids.

www.cicff2008.org

New York International Children's Film Festival

The New York International Children's Film Festival (NYICFF) was founded in 1997 to promote intelligent, passionate, provocative cinematic works for ages three to eighteen and to help inspire more compelling film for kids. Since its launch, the event has grown to become the largest festival for children and teens in North America, with a paying audience of over 20,000 attending the most recent event. Each year NYICFF presents a highly selective slate of the best animation, live action, documentary, and experimental film from around the world. The three-week festival presents films in competition plus gala premieres, retrospectives, filmmaker Q&As, workshops, receptions, and the NYICFF Awards Ceremony. NYICFF also presents screenings and premieres throughout the year at the IFC Center and other locations.

www.gkids.com

Los Angeles International Children's Film Festival

The Los Angeles International Children's Film Festival (LAICFF) showcases more than 100 films from around the world made for children and teens—animation, live-action, and documentaries—along with filmmaker appearances, animation and filmmaking workshops, and more.

www.lachildrensfilm.org

The Ottawa International Animation Festival

Founded in 1975, the Ottawa International Animation Festival (OIAF) was first held August 10–15, 1976. It created a gathering place for animation professionals and enthusiasts in North America. The OIAF is committed to ensuring the animation profession benefits from exposure to outstanding creativity and originality of emerging work, and young animators gain access to the movers and shakers of their chosen profession.

The Ottawa International Animation Festival
Ste. 120, 2 Daly Ave., Ottawa, ON K1N 6E2, Canada
www.awn.com/ottawa

Conventions and TV Marketplace Events

The events listed below are designed to introduce projects and production companies to the buyers. For getting everyone in the room together at the same time, these opportunities can't be beat.

Comic-Con

The San Diego Comic-Con is the country's premier comics and popular arts convention with an annual slate of special guests, themes, and programming.
www.comic-con.org

The KidScreen Summit

The KidScreen Summit is the largest and most important event for kids' entertainment executives. In 2007 the conference broke attendance records by attracting more than 1,300 delegates from thirty-eight countries.

Decision- and deal-makers in the kids' entertainment business attend to engage in critical dialogues on issues that affect the industry; take advantage of some of the industry's best networking opportunities; recognize and understand current market needs, opportunities, and challenges; learn more about key innovators and their vision; and find and share ideas that will drive their businesses forward.
www.kidscreensummit.com

MIPCOM

MIPCOM is the global content event for creating, co-producing, buying, selling, financing, and distributing entertainment content across all platforms. It provides the key decision-makers in the TV, film, digital and audiovisual content, production, and distribution industries with the only market conference and networking forum through which to discover future trends and trade content rights on a global level.

www.mipcom.com

MoCCA Art Festival

The Museum of Comic and Cartoon Art's annual MoCCA Art Festival allows attendees to meet comics and cartoon artists in four full ballrooms of cartoonists and publishers over three days of entertaining and educational panel sessions.

www.moccany.org/artfest-main.html

Red Stick Festival Pitch Contest

The Annual Red Stick International Animation Festival offering, Red Stick "Pitch!," provides the chance to pitch show ideas to a team of top sales and acquisition professionals from companies such as Nelvana, Corus Entertainment (Canada), MTV (USA and International), Cedecom (Spain), Beyond International (Australia's largest distributor), Trade Media (France), and many others.

www.redstickfestival.org/main/menu/pitch

Television Animation Conference

Every year, the Television Animation Conference (TAC) brings together key players in the animation industry from across North America and the world to the Fairmont Chateau Laurier as part of the Ottawa International Animation Festival (OIAF). TAC is the only trade forum in Canada that is specifically designed to bring together animation producers and buyers in order to provide them with a market for active networking, practical information exchange, and trade.

http://ottawa.awn.com/index.php

Animation Pitching and Development Bookshelf

The only thing you have to risk with these books, which should be a part of any creator's or development executive's library, is the occasional paper cut.

Hollywood Cartoons: American Animation in Its Golden Age by Michael
Barrier (Oxford University Press, 2003)
Kids Who Laugh: How to Develop Your Child's Sense of Humor by Dr.
Louis Franzini (Square One Publishers, 2002)
The Tipping Point by Malcolm Gladwell (Back Bay Books, 2002)
Prime Time Animation by Mark Harrison (Routledge, 2003)
Seven Minutes by Norman Klein (Verso, 1996)
Your Career in Animation: How to Survive and Thrive by David B. Levy
(Allworth Press, 2006)
Of Mice and Magic by Leonard Maltin and Jerry Beck (Plume, 1987)
Crafting a Cartoon by Joe Murray (e-book available at *www.joemurraystu-
dio.com*, 2008)
The Animation Business Handbook by Karen Rauqust (St. Martin's Press,
2004)
You Are Special: Neighborly Wisdom from Mister Rogers by Fred Rogers
(Running Press Miniature Editions, 2002)
Playing the Future: What We Can Learn from Digital Kids by Douglas
Rushkoff (Riverhead Trade, 1999)
How to Write for Animation by Jeffrey Scott (Overlook TP, 2003)
The Moose That Roared by Keith Scott (St. Martin's Griffin, 2001)
Original Cartoons: The Frederator Studio Postcards 1998-2005, edited by
Fred Seibert and Eric Homan (Easton Studio Press, 2005)
Producing Animation by Catherine Winder and Zahra Dowlatabadi (Focal
Press, 2001)

Legal Resources

Because animation pitching and development isn't just fun and games.

Volunteer Lawyers for the Arts

Since 1969, Volunteer Lawyers for the Arts (VLA) has been the leading
provider of pro bono legal services, mediation services, educational
programs and publications, and advocacy to the arts community in the
New York area. Through public advocacy, VLA frequently acts on issues
vitally important to the arts community in New York and beyond. VLA
is supported in part by public funds from the National Endowment for
the Arts, the New York State Council on the Arts, a State Agency, and the

New York City Department of Cultural Affairs, as well as through generous gifts from law firms, corporations, foundations, and individuals.
Volunteer Lawyers for the Arts
1 East 53rd St, 6th floor, New York, NY 10022
PHONE: (212) 319-ARTS (2787); FAX: (212) 752-6575

Canadian Intellectual Property Office

www.cipo.ic.gc.ca

U.S. Copyright Office

www.copyright.gov

About the Author

David B. Levy is the author of the successful book *Your Career in Animation: How to Survive and Thrive* (Allworth Press, 2006), which was the first career guide for animation artists working in North America. Levy has been an animation director for six series to date, including *Blue's Clues*, *Blue's Room*, *Pinky Dinky Doo*, *The Electric Company*, and *Assy McGee*. On his own, Levy has completed six award-winning independent animated films, including, most recently, *Owl and Rabbit Play Checkers*. His previous short, *Good Morning* (2007), has been featured in many film festivals, including the Hiroshima International Animation Festival and The New York International Children's Film Festival. Levy has served as President of ASIFA-East (the New York chapter of ASIFA International) since September 2000. He teaches animation at Parsons School of Design, The School of Visual Arts, and New York University's Tisch School of the Arts. He regularly lectures at Pratt Institute and the Rhode Island School of Design. In 2007, Levy signed a development deal for his own series creation and developed a TV property for an independent producer. Levy is married and lives in Brooklyn, New York.

Index

Page numbers in italic type refer to captions.

Books from Allworth Press

Allworth Press is an imprint of Allworth Communications, Inc. Selected titles are listed below.

Marketing Illustration: New Venues, New Styles, New Methods
by Steven Heller and Marshall Arisman (paperback, 6 × 9, 288 pages, $24.95)

Starting Your Career as a Freelance Illustrator or Graphic Designer, Revised Edition
by Michael Fleishman (paperback, 6 × 9, 272 pages, $19.95)

Inside the Business of Illustration
by Steven Heller and Marshall Arisman (paperback, 6 × 9, 256 pages, $19.95)

Business and Legal Forms for Illustrators, Third Edition
by Tad Crawford (paperback, 8½ × 11, 160 pages, $29.95)

The Education of an Illustrator
edited by Steven Heller and Marshall Arisman (paperback, 6¾ × 9⅞, 288 pages, $19.95)

Teaching Illustration: Course Offerings and Class Projects from the Leading Undergraduate and Graduate Programs
edited by Steven Heller and Marshall Arisman (paperback, 6 × 9, 288 pages, $19.95)

Your Career in Animation: How to Survive and Thrive
by David B. Levy (paperback, 6 × 9, 256 pages, $19.95)

Animation: The Whole Story, Revised Edition
by Howard Beckerman (paperback, 6⅞ × 9¾, 336 pages, $24.95)

The Education of a Comics Artist
by Michael Dooley and Steven Heller (paperback, 6 × 9, 288 pages, $19.95)

The Business of Being an Artist, Third Edition
by Daniel Grant (paperback, 6 × 9, 352 pages, $19.95)

Legal Guide for the Visual Artist, Fourth Edition
by Tad Crawford (paperback, 8½ × 11, 272 pages, $19.95)

Licensing Art and Design, Revised Edition
by Caryn R. Leland (paperback, 6 × 9, 128 pages, $16.95)

Successful Syndication: A Guide for Writers and Cartoonists
by Michael Sedge (paperback, 6 × 9, 192 pages, $16.95)

Mastering 3D Animation, Second Edition with CD-ROM
by Peter Ratner (paperback, 8 × 9⅞, 352 pages, $40.00)

To request a free catalog or order books by credit card, call 1-800-491-2808. To see our complete catalog on the World Wide Web, or to order online for a 20 percent discount, you can find us at **www.allworth.com**.